Who Decides Who Decides?

How to start a group so everyone can have a voice

by Ted J. Rau

Sociocracy For All
Amherst, MA USA
sociocracyforall.org

Sociocracy For All

Sociocracy For All

120 Pulpit Hill Road, Unit 8
Amherst MA, 01002
United States of America
info@sociocracyforall.org

Published by Sociocracy For All. Sociocracy For All is a project of Institute for Peaceable Communities (IPC), an incorporated 501(c)(3) non-profit organization in Massachusetts, USA.

Rau, Ted J., 2021   Who decides who decides? How to start a group so everyone can have a voice/Ted J. Rau.
    Includes diagrams, illustrations and references.
    ISBN 978-1-949183-04-7

Cover design: Klassic Designs
Illustrations: Ian Massey

Contents

"Ted Rau has done an outstanding job of tackling how to avoid the sneaky slide into a power struggle amongst well-meaning people who really want to cooperate and collaborate but need better tools. A practical, accessible approach to decision-making, this book is an excellent handbook for groups wanting to fulfill a mission and not spend their time stuck in a decision-making quandary."

Dawna Jones, author, Decision Making for Dummies

"How does one start a completely self-governed group? Ted Rau is one of the most appropriate people to answer this question, because it is something he works on every day, not only in the organization of which he is the operational leader and co-founder, Sociocracy For All, but also accompanying groups and organizations (for profit and non-profit) that seek self-management and sharing of power. For those of us who work with him, he is a constant guide and reference due to his great knowledge, multiple experiences and the ability to explain things with clear, simple and with replicable materials. This book brings great clarity to those who accompany groups and who are part of them, since there are always common situations. Here, we will find concrete ways to be able to navigate and overcome them."

Nora Plaza, Consultant, leader of Sociocracia Práctica

"What I love about Ted's writing is that he speaks from the heart and from experience. Everything Ted discusses in this book he has tried and tested; and everything works! Our world seems to be moving through a phase of increasing division and rampant self-interest. Forming small groups that embody cultures of caring, empathy and 'power-with' rather than 'power-over' is a way for each of us to practice the skills that the world needs to move toward greater harmony. Well functioning small groups are a powerful piece of the more networked world we are creating. Ted is a gift to the world, and this book is a fantastic, practical guide to creating groups with the culture we need."

Paul Atkins, Prosocial.world

Gratitude

I am feeling gratitude to my fellow travelers in Content Circle, in particular, Rodger Mattlage, who has made a huge contribution to this book. Joe Brewer gave the impulse that made me sit down and write. Marcus Petz made substantial early edits.

I am grateful to the Publishing Circle of Shala Massey, Russell Baldwin, Sara Rodriguez for connection, action, and companionship. I still don't quite understand how the universe connected us right at the perfect moment. I guess it was meant to happen!

Sociocracy For All provided me with the countless interactions that have led to an understanding of the issues forming groups face.

Jerry Koch-Gonzalez takes for granted what is evident to him. Yet, he taught me so much just by being who he is.

1
Introduction

Why this book?

Can you launch a new group in 3 meetings and establish shared power and self-management? I think you can, if, in those three meetings, you define the purpose well and put the needed infrastructure and practices in place. This booklet shows in detail how to do that.

Any organization will have a particular DNA – power relationships, practices, ideas – as it starts, and that very DNA is tough to change retroactively. The best idea is to start on the right foot at the very beginning.

Any group can form itself using the template outlined in this book. It works especially well if the founders and early members want to grow and nourish an organization that gives every member a voice and that is effective. Why those two, voice and effectiveness? Because that's what makes an organization. An organization is an organized body of people with a shared purpose. So what matters in an organization is the people, the purpose, and how we organize it.

If you are part of a group that has already formed but has struggled to get off the ground – in particular, if people are arguing over how to decide who decides what – you might be able to re-launch your group using this book.

Many areas of our societies need change. The issues humanity is facing are too many to list in all of our sectors: environment and climate, education, economy, health, and well-being. The agency of one individual, no matter how powerful, is limited. The only way to change anything is to change things on a systemic level, which requires the cooperation of people, groups of people, and groups of groups of people!

So many groups form. And so many groups fade. What distinguishes those groups that grow and flourish from those that fade and fail? The success factors are well-studied, even though the lessons learned hardly make it into the design of those who start groups. That makes sense – groups form because people feel the urgency for change in an area of their attention, not because they are experts in how to start a group.

Someone who wants to start a school might be an expert in teaching, not in starting organizations. Yet, much about starting a school is unique to *starting an organization,* not pedagogy. Am I saying that only "experts" should start groups or that every new group should have a consultant to help? Not at all! Quite the opposite. I intend to give everyone just enough guidance to start groups that get off on the right foot. That way, everyone can focus on their strengths and expertise, may it be pedagogy, coding, gardening, writing, forming a community, or making things. My dream is to bring the skill of self-governance into every corner of society.

In writing this book, I am making the assumption that we start a group aligned with the principles of sociocracy, also known as Dynamic Governance. Sociocracy is a governance system born in the late 1970s in the Netherlands. It has not yet become the "new normal," and it is still relatively uncommon in mainstream organizing. However, this is changing quickly right now!

Sociocracy combines the roots of consensus decision-making from the Quakers with insights from natural systems and cybernetics, forming a robust and simultaneously flexible system that is extremely adaptable to any organization. It builds on consent as decision-making, a way to make decisions without coercion. It also builds on small groups of "human scale". Sociocracy has a strong focus on increasing the flow of information and connection – the elixir that makes us understand each other.

Only if we work in a decentralized, flexible, and deeply respectful way can we address our realities' complexities. And more and more people see that.

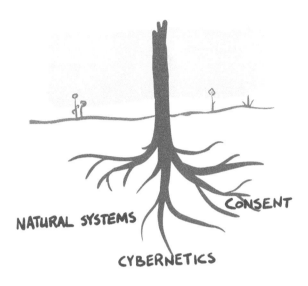

Who: new groups and early 'make-overs'

I wrote this book for everyone who deeply cares about a cause, and about collaboration as peers. Your cause might be the environment, equality, education. You might want to start learning pods, you might want to buy a store with others, or you might want to organize an online conference. Whatever your cause – if you are founding a group, this book will help you to set it up.

If you are part of a group that started a while ago and has been floundering, you can use this book to "re-launch" the group in a make-over with more clarity. For example, when I gave a copy of this book to a dear friend of mine who worked for a nonprofit organization of five staff that had been around for two years, he said, "Can I share this with my team? I think we still need to go through this process to understand how we're setting things up."

So if you're in this "operational but somehow not quite clear who decides" stage, you can use this book to give yourself a re-boot. However, you can only use the process in this book if the number of people actively involved in decisions or operations is ten people or less. If there are more than ten or twelve people involved already, and you do not know who decides and how, then this process will *not* be right for you. Note: if there are more people *tangentially* involved, it might still work. What matters here are the people who are under the impression that they are decision-makers and players in the group.

About the author

I am a full-time sociocracy trainer and consultant. Although I've had my share of starting groups – more often, I watch and support groups founded by others.

I myself do not join any group that doesn't meet my baseline:

- It has to be run sociocratically.
- It has to have a clear purpose that I find meaningful.
- It has to be with people I like.

Why would anyone do anything else? Without sociocracy, we will spend hours re-inventing governance, or we might re-invent top-down organizing. Without a purpose, we might disappoint each other or waste our time, and why do anything if it's not meaningful? Spending time with people I enjoy is a big motivator. With all the different directions we find ourselves pulled towards, connection is what adds the magic sauce.

A bit more about me: Born and raised in Germany, I hold a Ph.D. in linguistics (I wrote about on the interface of syntax and semantics). I live in an intentional community in Massachusetts that runs sociocratically. I am transgender and parent of 5 queer kids. I write music.

I enjoy where I am right now. I am content doing something that I am good at in an organization where I can be of service, together with mission-aligned people, for something that is needed and that is in increasing demand: supporting effective and egalitarian governance.

Born in 1979, I was born into a generation that was still processing the collective experience and traumas of fascism. I realized around the age of 13 that if so many people in a society can be so out of integrity, I myself couldn't be sure that I would do anything differently had I been in their situation. The mercy of having been born later was very real to me. I was able to grow up 'non-guilty' (at least of injustices of the past) only because I was born into a time when I didn't have to make those choices. It was then, as a young teenager, that I understood that systems are more potent than good intentions. In order to be who we want to be, we need systems around us that *support* our integrity, best intentions and allow for us to act accordingly. That's what governance is.

2

Context

What could possibly go wrong?!

To get tuned into that early stage of an organization, let me tell you stories about organizations that *didn't* make it.

I was talking in a Zoom call with two members of a group in Michigan. They had been part of an initiative for about two years that wanted to combine farming and living together. The handful of founding members had welcomed new members with open arms, and the "family" grew and grew. They decided things together. The group members deeply loved and respected each other – that was palpable even for me in listening to their story.

Over time, the more people joined, the harder and harder it got to hear everyone, despite everyone's friendship and best intentions. It was simply too many people. It became obscure who knew what, who wanted what for what reason, and who was doing what. It was nobody's fault; it was just a matter of bandwidth. As a result, decisions were slowed down. People weren't able to track each other's needs as well anymore. Little things were dropped here and there. And it was just a matter of time until some people started to interpret malicious intent into that unanswered email, that forgotten agenda item, that phone call that was never returned, that slightly misrepresented report. Tensions grew, and all of a sudden, love was not the answer to everything anymore. A system was needed. That's when they contacted me. But that didn't diminish the chaos. In that phone call, they told me this: "We all agree that we want to hire you to help us with our decision-making. But we don't know how to decide who decides to hire you." I never heard from them again.

The catch-22 nature of the problem made me squirm. They knew what I knew: that there was hardly any hope. Note again that everyone had the best intentions. The complexity of their problem had outgrown them. It was a checkmate kind of situation. I don't know how their story ended but having seen many similar stories, it is easy to imagine what happens next. Some people leave, in particular, those who want to help make things happen. Some people stay because they like the people or simply don't have a similar project in their lives that fills the gap. No new members join because everyone can easily sense that this organization is in trouble. It will fade away and die.

I find these situations disheartening. It is baffling that good intentions and affection don't seem to be enough to hold an organization together through growth. I wish it would, but evidence shows me that it simply is not true. An organization brings a level of complexity and dynamic that most of us are not prepared for. And that way, we walk into a trap – at least if we prefer to work in non-hierarchical ways.

That group could have been a growing family business, a non-profit, an activist group, a consulting firm – the dynamics are just what happens, like a play where all the roles are already set. It is pre-scripted because everyone does what makes sense in their position. The dynamics at play are bigger than what any one individual can change.

In some organizations, things play out differently. They slide down the slippery slope of 'more order means more hierarchy.' Let's look at an example.

A group of activists is forming a consumer co-op. Five families start buying almonds and tropical fruit together. They are well organized. Other families join in, and the group grows. Every other Saturday is busy now, sorting and packing and delivering. There's bookkeeping to do, and there are emails to send. Now those five families hold regular jobs, and some of them have children. They love their project, and they are proud of how successful and attractive it is as operations get more and more draining – a 'problem' of success. One group member happens to lose their day job, and they

finally decide that she could be in charge of leading operations. The project manager is now paid, and as she gets overloaded, more people get hired, starting with a bookkeeper. What started as a group of equals turns into a hierarchical organization like any other. After all, what other way was there, given that things needed to get taken care of? Five years later, some of the original members might still be around. But over time, the organization hardly even resembles what they so dearly cared for in the beginning.

(The plot might have changed slightly had the group set up a cooperative ownership structure early. But in the end, even big cooperatives very much resemble corporate structures in their decision-making. Although their ownership structure is different, their governance system for day-to-day operations looks the same.)

Another story. It was a group of people doing good work to create more local connections and infrastructure. Everyone was experienced, dedicated, and interested in the best for the group. Because everyone trusted each other, it seemed like not a lot of structure was needed. Similar to the first story, they ran on good intentions. So far, this group very much resembles the first story, but there is one big difference. One of them, Brian, was the founder. A charismatic and peer-oriented leader, he had gathered his friends around this project, who then brought friends. But in the group's

14

origin story, it was clear that this was "Brian's group" because of the effort and care he put into the project. Brian knew about sociocracy and knew that he wanted to give the project structure. He announced there would be teams (aka circles), and a lot of energy came from that. Yet, he wanted the group to have a say on the circle structure, which created a slowdown because it was hard to wrangle the group into giving feedback on the proposed structure. I am not quite sure what happened next. Maybe there were some hurt feelings. Something was said that wasn't received the way it had been intended. The next time Brian and I talked, resistance had started to form. People were demanding a say in what the structure would be and that Brian would not be the one who decides about the structure. But unfortunately, there was no structure in which to decide whether Brian could decide. Brian's proposal for a circle structure was met with rebellion. The group fell apart. I was shocked. In my view, Brian had done everything right. He saw the need for structure, and he made sure to implement it. He had asked for feedback. He was respected and experienced and not at all a power-grab kind of person. Quite the opposite! He had worked so hard to develop a suitable structure to distribute power because he had no interest in holding power. But he had waited too long. The group did not see that the only way to have power was to receive and accept it from the willing founder. The whole project withered away within weeks.

A lesson we can learn from this story is that **leadership is needed to distribute power.** Another national organization suffered the same dynamics, with an intense level of pain and suffering for everyone involved. The centralized organization leaders were not willing to distribute power, but they were also not holding it. Their excuse: "We're not holding on to power, quite on the contrary! There are so many decisions we didn't make that there's plenty of room for groups to step up." Yet, of course, that's not how groups step up. Distribution of power does not come from leaving a vacuum or letting things fall how they fall. Distributing power is an active process that requires listening, alignment, and skill. And that's what this book is about.

The question of legitimacy

Legitimacy is a sticky concept, especially in self-governance. If a group wants to self-govern, who decides that it will, and how?

In some models, it is the founder, or the owner of a company that puts the constitution in place to "make everyone equal under the constitution." Yet, could the person who puts it into place also take it away, like a parliament that operates at the mercy of a king?

Real self-governance is by the people and for the people. It is not put in place by anyone except the collective – otherwise, it could be taken away again.

A group of people needs to give itself a governance system, and the group needs to own and approve the governance system itself. Yet, there's a severe chicken-egg issue here – how can we take an unordered group of people and get them to follow a process to accept an orderly governance system?

Don't get me wrong – some groups manage. Yet, retrofitting an organization requires training, reflection, and conversation to collectively come to the insight that it's necessary and desirable to make the switch together. If just one person – in a consensus model – or one person with absolute power – in a hierarchical model – says no, then the way to self-governance is blocked.

16

So while retrofitting an organization with a collective organizing effort is possible, it's a bit of a gamble. That's why this booklet is taking an alternative approach. The idea is not to disregard those efforts – transforming organizations is still useful. But the more promising approach is this: can we plant the seed in a way so we can avoid all of these issues altogether? How does one *start* an entirely self-governed group?

A sociocratic organization holds a balance between all the different bodies – the circle members are balanced through consent. No one circle member can overpower another. The same is true for two circles in relation to each other – as we will see, linking and consent as well as aims (that are decided by consent) keep the balance between circles. No circle can ever overpower another circle.

Yet, if there is no organization yet, who decides who can join?

The question of where to start is a bit like asking, "how do you get two people onto a see-saw when they can't both get on at the same time?" Ultimately, one side might start and then let the other side get on. That's when the game begins. Alternatively, both can agree to hold the see-saw and coordinate to get on simultaneously. Both paths are combined in this book. The group of founders gets on together, creating balance for future members.

If there is one initial "creator" of the organization, then the legitimacy comes from there. That might happen if, for example, a grant giver calls an organization into existence, if an organization forms a spin-off or if a respected and quick-acting founder puts an organization in place and withdraws from the operations. Brian from the previous story could have created this scenario had he acted earlier and had it been clear that he will not interfere with the organization operationally. The chicken-egg issues around legitimacy don't tend to arise when that happens. People will accept that the organization has been formed that way and hopefully never question its origin.

However, the second scenario – a working group forming by itself – is much more frequent and is much more likely to stir up questions. It's the cooperatives, start-ups, activist groups, and all worker- or member-run initiatives that run into the legitimacy issues. It's almost impossible to create balance once everyone is already on the see-saw, plus there will always be battles over who got on first. This booklet focuses on those scenarios and shows to start without breeding resentment or raising suspicion.

Additional trouble?

Besides issues of legitimacy – which would already be bad enough, more issues make it hard to form a group:

- Most forming groups are short on financial resources and time. They can't just send everyone to get trained.
- Most forming groups are still learning how to execute the tasks and operations in their work. They often need to make a lot of operational decisions and get overwhelmed.
- Trust. A forming group might be a group of people who don't know each other yet. And even if they are familiar with each other, they likely need to re-establish a new kind of relationship, from friendship to co-worker or neighbor and co-owner. In either case, trust needs to form, and a track record of trust needs to build.

It is hard to get an organization off the ground and easy to fall into the trap of not deciding on our governance method because we don't have a decision-making method. Given that, shouldn't we make it as easy for each other as possible?

Before we walk through the different steps of how to form or re-set a group to avoid these pitfalls, let's look at the value set of sociocracy, the self-governance system that forms the foundation of this method.

The essence of sociocracy

Sociocracy is a rich, comprehensive governance system featuring shared power and self-management.

Sociocracy consists of a combination of tools and processes:

- We distribute decision-making authority into teams of people that we call circles.
- The decision-making method for circle decisions is consent: that means a decision is made when no circle member objects to the decision. One objects to a decision when a decision negatively impacts how the circle can achieve its shared aim.
- Links connect related circles. Links are circle members who are members of two related circles and can carry information back and forth. They also balance the power relationship between the circles.
- Circles define roles to make sure all functions of their circle are executed. Circles choose by consent which member fills a role.
- Most circles use rounds – the practice of talking one by one – in their circle meetings.

While *Who Decides Who Decides* is intended to be an exhaustive source, if you are looking for a reference book on sociocracy, see our manual *Many Voices, One Song. Shared Power with Sociocracy* and our online resources related to *Who Decides Who Decides*, including demos and templates: www.sociocracyforall.org/whodecides.

A shared mindset with fundamental values

Sociocracy is a living, evolving, integrated system of values, principles, patterns, practices, and tools for self-governance with shared power designed for people who share a mindset of a world that is nurturing, respectful and inclusive. In this mindset, they choose to work together collaboratively to realize their visions in ways that balance the fundamental values of efficiency, effectiveness, clarity, inclusiveness, and respect while embracing, the realities of uncertainty, continual change, evolution, and growth.

This is the foundational context upon which sociocracy has been created and continues to evolve.

Begin with the aim in mind

In sociocracy, we call a group's overall purpose it's *mission*, and what it will actually do to fulfill its mission we call its *aim* or *aims*. Having clarity around your group's mission and aim(s) is a critical factor for your group's success, as is the group members' commitment to the mission and aim(s).

A group's shared sense of identity is also essential to the group's success. That success is a product of its commitment to its mission and aim(s) and the way of working.

Shared power, personal agency, & individual needs

We human beings have complex motivations and needs. We need to know that we are valued, fulfilled, and effective group members. We also know that diversity provides a wealth of ideas and possibilities, which is the basis for our saying that "every voice matters." We need a governance system that balances realizing the individual's needs with the group's needs. Not only do we want the organization to be successful but also each of its contributing members. The basic ingredients of that are trust, equivalence of voice, and defined authority so everyone can fulfill their responsibilities without having to continually check back with some higher authority.

Responsibility, authority, and stewardship

You can't act effectively if you don't have authority. You can't have authority without being accountable and responsible. Each person, role, and circle in a sociocratic organization has responsibility for clearly specified *domains* (for example, marketing, gardens, membership, finances, strategy, publications, training, buildings and grounds, work schedules, events, actions, campaigns), and is responsible to the other members of the organization for getting input and *feedback* for decision-making and for the overall stewardship of that domain.

Effectiveness, efficiency, and clarity

We all want to do the group's essential work, and not "waste" time in meetings. Therefore meetings need to be efficient and effective. Sociocracy provides proven patterns and practices for conducting meetings and making decisions that promote clarity for all participants and balances the needs for effectiveness and efficiency. These ensure that there is clarity about each of a meeting's overall agenda and each of its agenda items, and clarity about the processes for working on each agenda item while ensuring that every voice gets heard. Sociocracy also provides patterns and practices for delegating responsibilities clearly, so everyone knows who is doing what and where there are interdependencies.

Personal and organizational change and trust

Change is a constant; the world is changing, our organizations are changing, and we are changing. It is essential that we recognize, react to, and adapt to changing conditions of our organization. As long as we remain members of an organization, we need to be willing to prioritize the good of the organization. Conversely, since an organization is made up of its members, the well-being and effectiveness of its members matter. We, the organization and its individual members, are interdependent. Since we all depend on each other, our currency is trust.

Meetings & Decision-making

As you will see in detail in the chapters below, the nuts and bolts of making sociocracy work are in its patterns and practices around running meetings and making decisions based on the notions covered in the sections above.

Since we can never know for certain what will be the "best"

decision at any moment in time (nor can we always take the time to even try), every decision is made on a *good enough for now* and *safe enough to try* consent basis.

Associated with those slogans are the notions of our *range of tolerance* as the basis for our *consent*, taking precedence over our *personal preference*. This is where we weigh our commitment to the organization and our commitment to work with a decision that is aligned with the aim of the organization.

Feedback and review

There are two important parts of the "good enough for now" piece. One is getting input and feedback in the process of making a decision to understand its potential implications. The other is a term where we set a time to review each decision in light of the situation at that future time, as well as to consider any feedback about any conditions or metrics we wish to measure and then to see how it is going and make any adjustments.

Summary

Sociocracy is an ecosystem of shared purpose, effective action, and mutual growth. When applied consistently, sociocracy's core notions covered above comprise an ecosystem of shared purpose, effective action, and mutual growth. It empowers a group and its members to work effectively and efficiently to realize the group's mission and aims in an atmosphere that engenders trust, continuing growth, and fulfillment.

3

Invitation to the 1st meeting

In my ideal fantasy, you have a cause, and you're ready to invite others to form a group. You are about to send a message to a group of people inviting them to a first meeting. What do you write?

The most important part of this invitation is to set an expectation that is accurate and helpful. There is one thing you absolutely need to say: **What the proposed aim of the group is.**

Must-have: the proposed aim

The aim has to be specific, to give people a clear idea of what project you are inviting them to. Let's say, for example, you want to form a climate group. You send an email to all your friends who care about the climate and invite them to the first meeting. Now you have ten people in the room. One of them has worked in climate research for 15 years and loves to geek out about statistics. Another cares more about biodiversity than climate. (Of course, the topics are related but still.) Yet another just recently caught on after their first child was born. They started to think, "as the child grows, how will climate change disrupt the world?" They aren't really interested in science but more in implications for their kids and climate education. Imagine their conversation - what common ground will they have?

You get the idea – 'climate group' is too big of a container. Your invitation was too broad.

Let's imagine you are throwing a party. You would never say, "I am inviting you to a party next week! See you then!" People would have no idea how to join your party, and that's what happens if the aim is too broad. A proper invite is specific, and if you're planning something particular, you should say so. For example, tell people if it's a costume party or a formal dress party. Tell them if it's a birthday party or a surprise party for your partner. People can choose to come or not – but not setting the terms is doing everyone a disservice. You don't get the party you wanted, and guests will be uncomfortable. A good host sets the stage so people feel comfortable and welcome. That's your job if you start a group.

Another factor is to manage the expectations: some groups are action-oriented, some are more for mutual support or learning. A climate group might be planning actions or talking about how to lobby or start a local chapter of a national climate organization. You might just want to grieve together and not "build" anything. Then grieving together is your aim. (Of course, any group's purpose might change over time, but then that's a decision that is made together and explicit.)

A specific invitation might sound like this: *I want to form a local chapter of the XY movement focusing on local activities that raise awareness about the climate and loss of biodiversity.*

The aim needs to describe what people will see you do when you are working on your project. Another way to describe it is, what's your product or your service?

Not setting a clear aim is the biggest mistake one can make. Once the group has bonded, people will have a hard time leaving it again – there is always inertia around leaving a group, and people feel bad when they do. Ultimately, without a defined aim, the group will spend months trying to determine its aim. At least one-third of the people will have joined with different expectations and will get more and more disappointed over time. The group might split. There will likely be hard feelings. Starting with an unclear aim is not worth it.

Can't the group decide the aim together? Probably – but it requires skill and focus. And what do you do if you have people in
the room that did show up with other expectations? Only leave the
aim up to the group if you are willing to tell people: sorry, it looks
like we have three different sets of expectations here. Let's split the
group. I think that it's too risky to gamble with people's time and
hopes.

Ultimately, any action means focus, which will mean letting go
of some alternative project one *could* have pursued. If that is hard
for you, this might help: there is space in the world for many wonderful opportunities. Not all of them will happen with me, that's
for sure! So if you have to say *no* to project C in order to focus on
projects A and B, just remember that you can wholeheartedly wish
project C all the best. By choosing projects A and B, you are not
saying that project C *isn't* worth doing. All you are saying is that
you will do projects A and B. It is not a rejection – even though it
might feel like one. Project C will flourish once it finds its place.
Just trust that it will.

Let me talk about a few common mistakes when writing an aim.

- Too many details. Don't say "growing the local gardening community by publishing a newsletter, managing a listserv, offering webinars, offering meetups, sharing articles in the email group, inviting each other to our garden tours, teaching how to make gardening zines, hosting weeding parties, connect local tree cutters with local gardeners, buying seeds together, sharing starters for those who have too many."

  Instead, say: "networking local gardeners for exchange of information, supplies, and support on physical tasks."

- Vague language. Don't say: "exploring the enhancement and stewardship of the interdependence between community members and their ecosystem." Instead, say: "organizing community events and meetups in Amherst to exchange information and practical tips on sustainable gardening."

Preparing for the aim: What if you don't know what aim people might go for? What if you can't decide? Does it seem like too big of a decision? In that case, I recommend some of the following options:

- Call each person on your invite list and get their input, ideas, and reactions.
- Run a study group or any kind of informal gathering that informs the aim for a founding meeting. It might take more than one attempt to hit the right spot.
- You might have to do several rounds of wording the aim and getting feedback.

Be aware that many of your ideas might not come to fruition. The focus of this book is not to help you brainstorm what kind of group might work out. The focus is on leading you to a self-organizing group once you know the aim.

Whatever it takes to get there, do not invite people to a _founding meeting_ until you have the aim proposal defined and clear.

A manageable group size

The processes in this book are going to work the best if your origin group is manageable. A group size of five or six people is ideal. Nine or ten pushes it. A group size bigger than that risks making the launch too hard, and then the group might fizzle out and fade away.

One key aspect of self-management is that it works best when group sizes are small so people can hear each other well. In a group of twenty people, in a two-hour meeting, only _some_ voices will be heard. That means you will set a culture where only _some_ voices count. In a small group, all are heard.

What about the people who are 'left out' because they are not invited? Ideally, invite a "first wave" of people first to keep the group size manageable. The group will be ready to hold a "second wave" and "third wave" later. If you respect them, prepare the ground well, and then include them into a welcoming organization where their voice will count.

While this book is strictly talking about an organization's operational part, there is a place for a wider network of people who aren't working but loosely connected. See the section on network

and community on page 91 to see how to keep a large number of people in the loop who want to support your effort but aren't direct contributors.

Explain your process

In your invitation, give people some information about how the group will be run. It would be a good idea to share the process in this book with people in your group. There are two reasons for it:

- Effectiveness: The more transparent you are, the easier it will be for people to join you in your efforts.
- Distribution of power: if you have a shared reference point on how to run your group, it won't all come from you as founder, which can help dilute a concentration of power.

You might announce what decisions you will make in the first meeting. We'll get to that, but for now, you could say something like, *I'd like to start a homeschooling co-op in our county that is based on outdoor education and runs 3x/week. Would that be of interest to you? If we want to start such a group, we need a good process in place to make sure we can include all the voices in the room so all members will run it as peers. [If you're curious about what I have in mind, you can read about the process I intend to use on www.sociocracyforall.org/whodecides. If we all know how it works, we can have clarity on how to get there.] The good thing about the template is that you can override anything you want to change. I can't wait to hear what you might have to contribute! Let me know whether you want me to invite you to the founding meeting."*

To invite people in, send the agenda to everyone who said they'd join at least 24 hours before the meeting.

The fact that you are organized and have a plan will show to them that you care about progress and about holding a container so people can be heard. The more convincingly you set the stage like that, the more likely people will be to step up themselves.

The template in the following chapter is not meant to be prescriptive. It's an offer. While I think the process is good as is and hope you give it a try, the integrity, purpose, and autonomy of your group are more important than following a set process. Yet, remember that good intentions aren't enough. To keep the balance between a robust process and flexibility to adjust to your context, my suggestion is to try the process as intended and adjust if necessary.

4

The first, founding meeting

You have a group of people in a physical or virtual room, and now it's time to get to know each other and launch!

Opening and consent to agenda

If you care about hearing everyone from the get-go, you need an intentional meeting format. Every group member should be able to access the agenda to be at ease. People can only follow your plan if they know your plan, and having it in front of them makes a big difference. If you haven't shared the agenda yet, share it at the beginning of the meeting. If you already shared it before the meeting, remind people where to find it or share it again.

This is the suggested meeting format:

Phase	Topic
Opening	Check-in
	ADMIN
Content	Consent to agenda
	Agenda items
	Update backlog
Closing	Check-out

The grey and white items are the scaffolding that holds everything in place – they are the same every meeting. The teal section is where your unique agenda items go, and we'll get to that.

Focusing on the overall format at first, below is what those parts mean. (You can find more details and examples in the sociocracy manual *Many Voices One Song*, Chapter 5, How To Run A Sociocratic Meeting.)

Check-In/opening round

A check-in is simple: do one round where everyone shares how they are doing entering the meeting. It can be simple and non-dramatic, "I am ok, a bit short on sleep. I had a meeting earlier that went pretty well, and I'm excited to be here and see what's going to happen."

If people know each other well, they might start sharing more vulnerably, which is connecting. (It might make sense to let those go first who have experience with check-ins.)

If people don't know each other at all, at this first meeting, ask people to say a bit about their background. They can share whatever might be relevant to the topic of your meeting. (Also announce that there will be a chance to share more about the personal experience, so it's ok to keep it brief for now.)

One comment that might be more of a personal preference of mine: I find check-ins the most relaxing and welcoming when the facilitator calls on people one by one and does so in a round, so it's obvious who will speak when.

Why not let people volunteer and speak at will until everyone has spoken? Or ask one person to go first and then have them name the next person? Well, here's how those formats land on me. In the first variant, I get so worried to awkwardly interrupt someone that it makes it hard for me to speak at all. In the second, I fear that moment of embarrassment when I name someone to go after me who has already spoken. That's why I save my guests the trouble and simply call on everybody one by one. Everyone will get to speak, and everyone will feel more comfortable when safely held.

ADMIN

The ADMIN part intends to clear all logistics out of the way. That way, we will be distraction-free later. This part will become more important over time. It's a good idea to establish it now and then build on that later.

Here are the different parts of the ADMIN part. Notice that their first letters form the word A.D.M.I.N. in English as a mnemonic and mental aid to memorizing all the parts.

Attendance. Notice who is there, and who isn't and make sure all the meeting-related roles are filled.

- Mention people who might be missing/late but are intending to join later. The people present will pick up that this group cares when people are missing and will appreciate that.

- As for roles, make sure to ask someone to take notes as minutes – ideally in real time.

- I assume you are facilitating by default. Ask for consent explicitly (and mean it !), making it easy to object. As a mental frame, ask for consent to facilitate the first meeting the same way you'd ask for permission to serve. Getting permission will prevent people from claiming later that you forced yourself onto the group.

- If you asked someone to facilitate, they ask for consent.

Duration. Set an expectation of how long you expect the meeting to be. My agenda proposal plans for circa two hours of meeting time. Some people might tell you now that they have to leave early. Good to know so we can plan realistically and adjust!

Minutes. This does not apply to the first meeting. In all future meetings, this is the place where we'd check whether all circle minutes are up to date and have been distributed to whoever needs to see them.

Information. Ask if anyone has any announcements they want to share. It could be just a piece of information, an invite, or a celebration. For a first meeting where people don't know each other, they will most likely not have anything to say. That's ok. Just by asking, people will now know that this is a place where one can bring announcements.

Next meeting. Maybe your group already has another meeting set up? If so, remind everyone when that is. If there is no new meeting set up, you can skip this and arrange the time, date, and location towards the end of the meeting.

Consent to agenda

The agenda in a sociocratic meeting is decided by consent. In my view, this is an innocent-looking step with huge importance. Please do not gloss over it or skip it.

How it's done: present the agenda with enough detail so people understand and form an informed opinion on whether the agenda will serve the group's purpose. Encourage people to ask questions – show that you care whether they understand. Then ask whether they see any reason to change the agenda or whether it is good enough to get started. If no one speaks up, you've now made your first consent decision as a group.

Why is this so important? Because the agenda is the agreement of how we spend our time together. That is a decision we make together. That means that everyone in the group is co-responsible for sticking to their own agreement. If later, for example, one person talks for 10 minutes at a time repeatedly and causes the agenda to run over, and that every person has consented to the original agreement, you now have something to hold them accountable to by reminding them that an agreement was made.

Consenting to the agenda together is crucial because you are not forcing an agenda onto the group. You are proposing, and the group is actively embracing it. Remember the see-saw? It's a bit like all your guests are standing around the see-saw, and you are asking for permission from everyone so you could hold it in place for a moment so we can all put the first foot onto the see-saw. And this is where it all begins.

Agenda items

Now you will start making decisions and talking about topics. I suggest the following agenda items for the first meeting:

(a) Decision to commit to consent and rounds
(b) Decision about the aim
(c) Exploration of experiences with regard to the aim
(d) Getting to know each other
(e) Decision on current membership
(f) Next meeting

I will discuss these topics in more depth later in this chapter, but I'd like to show how these topics follow a natural progression. (You are, of course, free to change the order of agenda items or to put some agenda items off until the next meeting.) Here are my thoughts on why these topics make sense in this order.

- In (a), we set the groundwork for any other decision. Before we have a **decision-making method**, we can't do anything. In the same way, **rounds** are a great way to keep discussions flowing and orderly, and inclusive. So before we can talk and make decisions, we need to establish how we do that. If you don't, your fate will most likely be like the organizations' in the section of "What could possibly go wrong?!"
- As the next step in (b), we define what we are doing. The **aim** is a description of that. If we have different expectations and intentions, it's best to hear this right away.
- In (c), we get to hear what kinds of **experiences or assets** people bring. It's a way to know what is even possible and as we start dreaming together.
- Topic (d) gives you a chance to learn more about the other people in the room. Knowing each other as human beings, a sense of **connection**, sets the foundation for collaboration.
- Topic (e): Now that everyone in the room has a sense of what the group will be like – how it will be run, what it will do, what we know as a group, and who the people are who are also in the room, everyone can make an informed decision.

Do I want to be a part of this? Are these the people I want to do it with? In other words, do I **consent to be a member**, and do I consent to the others being members of this group?

- Topic (f): Now that you know who is even part of this group, and you have more of a sense of what you need to do by when, **schedule another date.**

Committing to consent

A group that can't decide how to decide will struggle. It's a bit like you can't discuss what language you are going to speak without speaking in a language. It's circular, and that circle can easily be a death spiral.

There are a lot of decision-making methods. For example, you can vote by majority vote, but that would mean you'd have to be ok with ignoring 49% of the voices. You could use consensus (which will be very similar to consent), but it may set you up for lengthy discussions and might put the group at the mercy of individuals who block decisions.

Someone in your group might have heard about the advice process: that's when we empower individuals to make decisions after consulting with others. That's a great way to do things and very compatible with sociocracy. Yet, it's a secondary method of decision-making because it requires that we already made the decision somehow to empower that individual so that particular individual can decide. So that will be added later. For now, we are looking for a way our group can decide, not for a way how individuals can decide.

Consent

Consent is a decision-making method where a proposal is approved if no one in the group sees a reason to object. A reason to object would be that the proposal harms the aim of the group. If someone sees a reason, we work as a group to see if we can tweak the proposal until it does work. To approve a proposal, 100% of all group members need to consent.

Note that they don't have to love the proposal to consent. It's ok when the proposal is good enough and doesn't violate the aim.

When I try to give a quick-and-dirty impression of consent, I always tell the following story. You are welcome to borrow my story or find your own story:

I have five children, and they are all very different from each other. They like different things, and they dislike different things. Let's say I want to decide what to have for lunch. If I ask them, "what do you want for lunch?" then I lost already. There is absolutely no way these five individuals will ever want the same thing. And just by asking what they want, I have already set myself up for failure because they now assume that they can always get what they want.

Instead, I need to ask for ideas for lunch. Out of those ideas, I pick something and propose it. Let's say I want to propose burritos.

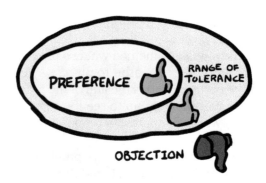

The question I need to ask then is *not*: "Do you want burritos for lunch?" The question is: "Is there any reason *not* to have burritos for lunch?"

That way, now the family member that has a reason not to eat burritos will be able to say so. But if one child really wanted noodles but is willing to go for burritos, we can still make a decision. I've set the expectation to what people are willing to do, not what they want to do.

(While this is an example that clicks well with people, family decision-making is tricky because families lack a clear and explicitly stated aim. Is the aim to spend time together or to support each other in a healthy way? I guess it's something like that, but it is different from an organization we join out of choice around the aim. Yet, it sure was quite a memorable moment when I realized that. It was on Main Street in the town where I live, about half-way between the pizza place and the burrito place, with two kids in a full-blown tantrum, and I swore to myself never to make that mistake again.)

Consent keeps things moving. If someone objects, the objections point out exactly what issue we need to focus on to improve the proposal. For example, let's say burritos are more expensive than pizza and the paying parent objects. Can we make a deal of getting the least expensive order? Or let's say one of the kids doesn't like spicy food. Can we order a non-spicy version? Objections are welcome to improve the proposal.

It's important to build some skills around consent. For example, "I don't want burritos" or "How about Chinese instead?" are not problems we can solve, so they are not productive. They will distract the group and need to be gently steered back to the question on the table (= "Is there any reason not to have burritos for lunch?") by the facilitator.

Don't get dragged down into rabbit holes here. The aim is what you will decide next, and yes, that gets very circular. You also don't know yet who is "the group," so all of that still needs to be defined. So, for now, try to stay on the topic of the decision-making process only. The question is only: how do we as a group approve a proposal? To consent to something means to say, "I can (and will) work with this."

When you introduce consent decision-making in your group, you might not go into that much detail. But maybe now you know what you can say in case someone questions your choice.

Step by step

In order to introduce the question, what I would do is to formally propose consent as a decision-making method.

- **Present the proposal and clarifying questions**. The proposal sounds like this:

  I'd like to make sure we know how we make decisions. I propose consent as a decision-making method. What I mean by that is that if we have a proposal, we would ask each person in the group if they are ok with the proposal. It just needs to be good enough for each member of the group. That way, we can make decisions more easily without arguing. If something isn't good enough, we will improve it together.

  Then you ask for understanding: does everyone understand what was proposed? Go slow – consent is only consent if you understand what you're consenting to!
- **Quick reactions.** Then give people a chance to give their reactions, ideally in a round. They might say things like, "I am curious what this will look like, but I am willing to give it a go," or "We also do that in our other group, so it sounds good to me."

- **Consent.** Then – drumroll – comes the magic moment. You now use consent as a decision-making method to implement consent. Ask everyone, person by person, whether they are willing to commit to consent as a decision-making method. If you're comfortable and that kind of person, this is a good moment for a joke because it sure is a bit awkward. Remember, it's the only way to make it onto that see-saw.

I assume that in most groups, everyone will consent. Yet, to prepare you – what objections or concerns might people have towards consent as a decision-making method?

They might be worried because they don't understand it. In that case, you may validate that you take their fear seriously and then offer training or more information.

They may be concerned that their voice won't be heard. So reassure them by reminding them that if they have objections to a decision in their circle, their voice will always be heard. Model that very promise by listening well and addressing what they are saying.

What if...?

What if someone doesn't want to accept this, no matter what? I would not even start working with anyone who is not willing to accept consent as a decision-making method and who is not willing to work out a proposal with me that would allow them to say yes to consent as a method. Let's say this person is only willing to operate by parliamentary procedure. If it's important to you to give a minority a say, then majority vote isn't good enough.

Even postponing the decision or a "trial version" is dangerous because then it is unclear how we are operating before and after our decision, and we might get stuck in limbo – which is precisely what we're trying to avoid. It would be like saying, "we'll talk in English for three months, and then we can use any language anyone chooses to talk about what language we'll speak in next." See how that doesn't work?

If it were me and there is a discussion on this topic, I would take my energy and ideas elsewhere. I urge you to do the same.

Committing to rounds

Rounds

While not as vital as consent, it makes sense to make one more agreement on how we operate: rounds.

The practice of rounds is simple. By default, we speak one by one until everyone has spoken once. Then we start again.

Rounds are a manifestation of the principle that everyone's voice matters. Rounds focus us because every round will have a prompt. That way, at any given point in time, we know what we are talking about. In that way, even though they seem lengthy at times, they save time overall.

By the way, doing rounds is different from speaking at will and then saying, "let's hear from the people who haven't spoken." While rounds presuppose that everyone's voice counts equally, the missing voices are an afterthought in the second scenario.

Not everyone has to speak in every round. Some people might pass and not speak when it is their turn; they still have had the same chance to speak as everyone else. In some rounds, like decision-making rounds (consent rounds), no one can pass because we need to know from everyone whether they consent or object.

Step by step:

Propose the use of rounds as a default way of working, for check-ins and check-outs, most explorations, and for consent rounds. This default can be overridden, for example, for brainstorming sessions, but that would have to happen intentionally.

Proposal: we commit to rounds as a default way of talking, in particular for check-ins and check-outs, most explorations, and for consent rounds.

As always with the full consent process, allow

- clarifying questions (in a round if you want)
- quick reaction round
- consent round

If I were you, I would certainly do a full round to hear everyone's consent, not only for the pun but also because of the self-commitment that comes with hearing everyone speak out loud.

What if...?

What if someone objects? The most typical reason is that people find rounds "rigid." Try your best to listen to what the basis of their objection is. Reflect it back to make sure they have been understood.

Most likely, it will be hard to predict whether the concern is connected to harm. It is probably true that the group may fulfill its aim both with or without rounds. What you can do is to offer a trial period, for example of three months. At the end of this trial period, people might have gotten used to rounds, or you might qualify when to do rounds and when not to do rounds.

(In case you're wondering why I am suggesting trial periods for rounds but not for consent, here is why. Let's go back to the comparison with speaking in a language: consent is a decision on what language we even speak. Rounds are an add-on, like speaking in rhymes (more wholesome!). Yet, we can break rhymes from time to time without failure of communication. It's good to do as much as possible but not a dealbreaker per se.)

What if someone breaks rounds because they forget? Nothing. There is no punishment. But having this shared commitment means we give those who want to create an even playing field the right to interrupt and steer the group back into rounds.

Approving the aim

Your aim

Ideally, the aim is what you used in your invitation, the description of what you are trying to do. As mentioned earlier, the aim should be specific and clear.

Technically, only an aim is needed to start a group. Most groups prefer to have a vision or mission statement for the bigger picture. In a mission statement, we raise the overall issue we want to address. The mission statement is the *why* of the initiative. The aim states *what* you're going to do, and that you need from the beginning.

We find that fill-in-the-blank statements work the best for groups:

We want to ... (MISSION) **by ...** (AIM).

Examples:

- *We want to empower elementary school children and strengthen their social connections by forming mentoring relationships between 5th-grade students and first graders.*
- *We want to increase the visibility of queer artists by crowdfunding and funding awards for young transgender and gendernonconforming artists in Western Massachusetts.*

- *We want to help regenerate the ecosystem in the XY bioregion by attracting and supporting (with skills, networking, and funding) example local generative projects.*

Choosing a shared aim is as crucial to an initiative as singing the same song is essential to singing together. You can't sing together if you can't agree on a song. To stay in that metaphor, it might well be that everyone sings a different *tune*. As long as it's coordinated and the same song, everything fits together and forms a whole. You *invited* everyone to sing a certain kind of song. Everyone invited who is intrigued shows up, and then you formally *propose and consent* to singing the song.

Step by step

You, as the convener, will probably have some part in writing the aim. Maybe you are writing it by yourself, maybe with others, or with others' input. You, as the facilitator, need to make sure an aim gets decided.

It's often too hard to word-smith the aim with a group so work with your prepared proposed aim as a starting point. Go into the regular consent process (see page 45) that you already know.

There might be amendments to the aim, like a change in wording or an addition. While that is ok, make sure not to water down the specificity of the aim. If you include every possible action into the aim, it becomes meaningless.

There might be objections. And that's where there is again some chicken-egg situation. Objections are typically evaluated with the aim as the backdrop. But there is no aim yet. So it becomes about every person's individual consent. You try to maximize the number of people that can say yes to an aim that is still meaningful and that you can act on.

What if...?

It is perfectly possible not to move forward. Maybe the needs and interests in the room are too diverse to fit into the same conversation. Going back to the aim as the song, you would not consent to

44

Understand the proposal
(here: the proposed aim).
Read it and allow questions.

Reaction round
Let everyone share thoughts
and feelings in a round.

Consent round
Ask everyone in a round
whether they consent or
object to the proposal (= the
aim).

singing three different songs at the same time, would you? Then don't cluster too many things into the same project, only those that mutually enhance each other.

What might be a sub-group of the same project and what makes the project too spread out to remain coherent is only for you to know. Take your own right to object or consent very seriously. If you compromise at this moment, you might regret it for years to come. It's like a relationship that you are entering into. Are you where you want to be?

The same, of course, is true for everyone else. And I know that this is hard. It might mean that someone you like and respect – and maybe worked hard to get into this room – is not on board on the same aim and will leave the project. Remember that someone who doesn't consent to the same aim might still remain connected, just not as a (decision-making) member of this group. They might cheer for your project from the sidelines, but they will not participate. That's ok.

Again, be present with every fiber of your body. Take every red flag and belly ache seriously. Only move forward if you feel that clean, "Yes, I consent!" inside of you. For your project's and your own sake, gift the group with the same honesty and integrity.

It might be a good idea to hold off questions of membership, i.e., who will join and who won't. For now, try to focus on what aim gives the project the best chances to be successful.

Exploration of experiences related to the aim

The hard work is almost over! This agenda item is fun!

What are you bringing?

In this agenda item, no decision is needed. All we need is sharing and listening. Most likely, everyone in the room has something they have to offer. Like in a gifting session, figuratively gather it all in the middle of the circle by doing a round where everyone shares, one by one, what they have to bring.

Step by step

Frame the question well. Restate the aim. Ask, "when you think about this project with the aim (...), what can you think of that you bring as a resource, like previous experiences, connections, contacts, and resources? Let's gather them all and make sure to write them down!"

Writing them down will be useful for the future. You might go back to that list later as new people have joined or the project focus has shifted or broadened. This list is your treasure box!

What if...?

In my experience, some people tend to sell themselves a bit over or a lot under value, especially along gender lines. If you sense that is happening, you might raise that issue. If there are cross-connections between the group members, but not everyone knows each other, it might be a good idea to have another round to add to others' list of resources. For example, let's say it is Michelle's turn, and she understates that she has written two books on the topic. Wait until Michelle is complete and then ask others what they know about Michelle that might be of use.

Getting to know each other

We are more than our expertise. Now that the hard work is done, relax, and tell each other some life stories. Who are you? What's important to you? A nice prompt that I use a lot is, "What are you passionate about?", or "What was your path to get here?". It's a sure win because it gives everyone a chance to shine.

If you think it will be necessary, set a timer for each person in the round. One can say a lot in 2 minutes if focusing on the relevant information!

The only 'outcome' for this topic is increased connection and sense of belonging. After all, it is really hard to see someone shine and not bond with them.

Defining the founding members

Knowing who you are

You now have decided on your basic governance set-up (consent & rounds). You know your aim, your group's resources, and the people behind it. Do you want to be part of this?

This is not just a formality. The group members that recognize each other as formal group members become the seeding group for everything else. In a way, they are giving each other (or themselves?) legitimacy.

That's where things get a bit funky again. Because now we are deciding – by consent, of course – that we are willing to work with each other.

Step by step

Set the context by explaining the situation. In an existing group, membership is approved by consent because a group needs to be able to decide who is a member. So if I want to join an existing group, the existing members of the group will need to consent to me joining.

Now there is a process and an aim but no people in it yet. You are consenting to each other to, again, step onto the see-saw together. It's weird, but we need this moment. Here is how you can go about it.

1. Explain the situation
2. Ask everyone to stand up or raise their hand or in some other way to indicate whether they want to be members of the group. Look around.
3. Ask for consent from everyone to everyone who indicated they wanted to be part of the group.
4. You are now a circle.

A possible objection might be that the group lacks experience in a certain area. Or that it's too many men, white people, or whatever might be relevant to your group.

If there are objections, remember that this is the beginning and not cast in stone. For example, if someone objects based on gender balance, there could be a term date by which you re-evaluate the gender balance, and you put a plan in place on how to add people to your group to create a better mix. Note that in this case, with the term end and evaluation date, we are still striving for consent for now (as in "good enough") and not putting off the decision. In that scenario, we would make ourselves members today but would commit to addressing the issue.

If in any way possible, **hold off on inviting others and just focus on group cohesion right now** until the second meeting. I am guessing this will be hard. Maybe there is that person that was planning to come and couldn't make it. But remember that this phase is critical for a good and robust launch. If new people join right now, I'd be worried that the commitments we made today get watered down.

(If it's one person or two, I'd personally be willing to compromise and – with everyone's consent – invite them to the next meeting. For example, if someone in the group commits to sitting down with the incoming member to explain what was decided, I'd be comfortable to consent.)

Can new members join the circle later? Yes, they can! However, I suggest that you wait until the second meeting to decide that.

Don't rush it – the principle of "the more, the merrier" can easily turn into "the more people, the less forward motion" if you don't have an agreement on how to go about it.

What if...?

What if, for example, you love the aim of the group, but you don't think that guy across from you has enough experience to join? Or if you're worried that this person's hardcode cynicism will make it harder to create a healthy group culture?

I know I am asking something almost impossible. After 2 hours with this new group, it's a tall order to tell someone that you don't consent to them being a part of the group. How could you?

Yet, I don't know what else to tell you. Only join the group if you are in integrity with yourself. If there is someone you are not willing to work with, find a place inside yourself that might give you the courage to address your concern. Maybe it is something that could be changed? For example, maybe that guy who talked so much could be told to hold his horses and listen more? I know it's hard, and I can't even promise that I would do it every time myself.

Just consider the alternative of having to work with someone whose performance chronically undermines the group's success. It's a non-starter. Do yourself a favor and speak up.

Before you object, ask yourself whether your bad feeling is "just" based on a preference or whether it will harm the project. You don't have to love everyone, and you're not getting married to the project – but you have to be comfortable enough to operate well. Only you can decide.

From the project's perspective, it doesn't matter how many people are in and how many are out. Once there is a group of at least two people, the project has officially launched with its first members.

The worst outcome, however, is if people stay vague about their membership. Any project can only take a small number of people "riding along" before the group gets drained. Ask everyone to make up their minds – maybe offering one-on-one conversations outside of the meeting. Or invite them to come back and join later.

Next meeting

Plan the next meeting with those who have just become members. Alternatively, decide on a method by which that decision will be made. Be sure to be specific – for example, make sure you know *who* will take on the scheduling.

Backlog items?

In talking, you might have come across open questions or topics that need more exploration. To build cohesion and coherence in the group, harvest those open questions at the end of the content pieces. We will gather future topics in the second meeting, so keep it simple for now – just notice what has surfaced that you want to capture. (For example, if you have committed to re-evaluating a decision later.)

Check out (meeting evaluation)

In a round, ask people how they feel about the meeting and what they would like to improve for the second meeting. It is quite likely that people will be too polite to say anything that needs changing, so be sure to explicitly express interest, for example, by saying, *I want to make sure our meetings are the best they can be. What did you enjoy in this meeting that we should do again? And what would improve your experience?* Take notes - if there are specific ideas or issues, add them to the backlog.

The reason we do this in a round is that it's already hard for most people to bring up something worth improving. By asking everyone to say at least one thing about the meeting, we might break the ice and hear a fuller range, not only the complaints or only the praise.

Summary table for meeting #1

I am assuming a group size of 3-9 people for this first meeting. This meeting agenda adds up to 120 minutes. Time should be manageable if you don't get lost but add new and tangential topics to the backlog. (See the appendix for a printable version.)

min	Topics	Description
15	Check-in	"Who are you, and how are you?"
5	ADMIN	Attendance, duration, (minutes,) information, (next meeting)
5	Consent to agenda	Describe the agenda and ask for consent
10	Topic #1	Commitment to consent
10	Topic #2	Commitment to rounds
20	Topic #3	Decision about the aim
10	Topic #4	Experience with regard to the aim
15	Topic #5	Getting to know each other
10	Topic #6	Defining the founding members
5	Topic #7	Next meeting
5	Update backlog	Anything you want to flag for later?
10	Check-out	"What was this meeting like?"

Follow-up

- Follow up on all the things you've promised
- Send the notes to everyone who attended
- Send a reminder and the agenda for meeting #2

5

The second meeting

You will now build some infrastructure for the circle, start shifting power away from yourself, make a plan on how to tackle the issues, and whether to invite new members. The second meeting follows the same format as the first meeting:

Phase	Topic
Opening	Check-in
	ADMIN
Content	Consent to agenda
	Agenda items
	Update backlog
Closing	Check-out

All you need to do is plug the agenda items from this chapter into the teal area where it says "Agenda items." The agenda items are:

- Selection: facilitator, leader & secretary
- Infrastructure and communication
- Gather items for the backlog
- Prioritize the backlog
- Add new members? (y/n)
- (Select new members)

Opening and ADMIN

The check-in for this meeting is the same as always: how are you? Most likely, everyone has had a busy day, so make sure to slow down and arrive and be present.

The ADMIN phase is now relevant in full. I am repeating some slightly changed info so that you have it all in one spot:

Attendance.

- Who is here, who is not? Who said they wouldn't make it, or they'd be late?

- Make sure all the meeting-related roles are filled. Ask someone to take notes until you select a secretary.

- You are again facilitating by default. Ask for consent to continue just for a few minutes until you have your official facilitator.

Duration. Set an expectation of how long you expect the meeting to be. The plan is set up for 120 minutes. Some people might tell you they are leaving early.

Minutes. Have the minutes been distributed? Did everyone receive them? (For example, did any emails bounce, etc.?) Is there consent to the minutes? An objection to the minutes would mean that something in the minutes is an inaccurate representation of what others perceived in the meeting. This is rare and so this should not take long. Find consent and move on.

Information. Ask if anyone has any announcements they want to share now.

Next meeting. Maybe your group already has another meeting set up? If so, remind everyone when that is. If not, schedule a meeting now or assign the task to someone in the group.

If any topic here sparks a discussion, either put the topic on the agenda or note it for later.

Consent to agenda

Present the agenda as laid out in this chapter (and in the summary table at the end of this chapter). Make sure people know enough to make an informed decision and ask for consent.

(While you are following a template, there might be reasons to adjust the agenda with additions or modifications. Note that if you're short on time or run out of time, today's last two agenda items can be moved to next time.)

Selecting roles

The first agenda item will be to select people into the three roles:

- leader (or use the term *coordinator*)
- facilitator
- secretary

Having those roles will make it easier for the circle to operate. Choosing the people who serve in those roles with intentionality will support equal consideration of everyone's needs and trust.

(Note: sociocracy's 4th standard role, the delegate which links to the parent circle, is not needed in a one-circle organization because there is no circle to link to.)

Define the role and the term

Before you can select anyone into any roles, people need to understand what the roles entail and how long a person will serve. By default, we suggest you use six months as a term.

The role descriptions on page 57 are intended as a starting point. If you want to keep things simple, just use them as they are; otherwise modify as needed. You can approve them using the regular consent process (see page 58).

Role	Activities
Leader	Making sure the circle is operating.

- Checking in with people and tasks
- Serving as 'catch-all' that notices items that are falling through the cracks and either deals with them or brings them to the circle.

Facilitator	Running circle meetings.

- Planning the agenda (with leader input) and inviting members.
- Holding circle meetings.

Secretary	Keeping the circle's documents in order.

- Taking notes and making sure minutes and other related documents are accurate and up to date.

SECRETARY   LEADER   FACILITATOR

Understand the role.
Read the role description.
Answer clarifying questions.

Reaction round
Give people a chance to give brief (!) reactions or amendments.

Consent round
Ask for consent to the role descriptions as they are stated. If there are objections, modify as needed.

Gather qualifications and get consent

Next, for each of the roles, compile a list of qualifications and qualities that a person filling that role should have, similar to the table on page 59. In rounds, let each person say one item until you run out of ideas. When the list seems ready, ask for consent. "Is this list good enough to base our decision on, and to go on to the next step?". You can check for consent by using hand signs like thumbs up.

Note down nomination

Ask every circle member to note down silently who they would like to nominate. Tell everyone that they can nominate themselves!

Ideally, everyone notes down their nominations for each role (like on paper or in a private message) so everyone can form their original idea without getting distracted by the others' opinions. There is value in people's original ideas, so let's hear them.

Role	Qualities and qualifications
Leader	• Good at tracking tasks • Good follow-up • Communication skills • Trusted by the group
Facilitator	• Experience/willingness to learn • Gentle but focused • Multi-partial (hold own opinion lightly)
Secretary	• Good at multitasking • Fast typing • IT skills

Nomination round

Ask everyone in a round to share who they nominate for which role and why. Ideally, reasons for nominations refer back to the qualifications. (Ask people to refrain from mentioning who they *don't* nominate because it's typically not useful to do that.)

Change round

After the nomination round, do another round where people can change their nominations. If they change their nomination, they may want to share new insights that led them to change their nomination. Be sure to let them know that it is not necessary to have full convergence – not everyone needs to nominate same person per role to continue.

Propose a candidate and find consent

The facilitator makes sure that a candidate is being proposed for each role. The easiest way to ensure that is to make a proposal.

Alternatively, the facilitator can ask someone else to make a proposal and ask for consent. For example, this could sound like this: "I propose that Michelle be the leader of this group for six months, I be facilitator also for six months, and Marco be the secretary for six months. Are there any objections? Remember that you object if you have reasons to assume that we can't fulfill our aim with that person in that role." (Find more details and examples in *Many Voices One Song*, Chapter 3.6.)

If there are objections, try to integrate. For example, if an objection is that someone might not have enough time, propose a different candidate, shorten the original candidate's term, or see if you can free that person up to serve this role. If the objection is that someone does not have enough experience, see if you can give them extra training or shorten the term.

Some groups try to rotate or split roles. Both of those strategies reduce the clarity of who does what. As an alternative, we recommend having short terms (like three months) so that more people can hold roles over time but the first 'officers' can grow into their role.

You now have a facilitator, leader, and secretary! Celebrate and thank them! They may start their job immediately or at the next meeting. Ideally, the facilitator is familiar with this booklet. If not, support them in following the process.

Infrastructure and communication

Each circle requires a little bit of infrastructure for circle documents and email addresses or handles. It creates unnecessary friction if the documents are all over the place or if some circle members are forgotten in our communication because we hit "reply all" in just too many different email threads.

So while this item might be small and easy, it's important nonetheless. To speed things up, you, as the convener, can bring a proposal to the meeting. Here is an example proposal for you to start from:

> This circle will communicate using email. Our secretary will create a … and make sure all members are

included. All circle documents (lists, minutes, and reference documents) will be in the ...folder (link). Within that folder, there will be one meeting minutes document that collects all minutes in the same document. At the top of that document will be the **backlog** (= the list of future agenda items) of the circle.
Term: 6 months

The idea is to be as clear and practical as possible with as little extra overhead as possible while finding a solution that includes all members.

For your proposal, follow the typical consent process of presenting the proposal/clarifying questions, quick reactions, and consent.

Once you have established the backlog, here are two items you can already put onto the backlog:

- selection process (date: whenever the terms are up that you've set in the selection process);
- review communication and circle documents policy (date; whenever the term is up that you've set just now)

Gather items for the backlog

The next task is fun again! You get to fill that backlog with a lot of exciting ideas!

Given your aim and expertise, what are the topics or questions you will have to address? Problems you will have to solve? By that, I mean concrete, doable things. It might help to prompt these by starting people off by saying, *"How might we...?"*

Do this in rounds. Ideally, every person offers only one or two at a time, and you do several rounds. That way, you can weave the circle member's interests together already, as people build on each other's ideas.

Have the secretary write those ideas into the backlog. That's where those backlog items will live until we can address them.

Prioritize the backlog

You can't do everything at once. And that's frustrating! Within your group, there might be disagreement on what needs to be dealt with first. Quite a few groups go down the unfortunate rabbit hole of arguing over what is more important. For example, I have witnessed groups that get slowed down because they could not decide whether to focus on topic A *or* B. Instead of making a plan of how to get *both*, they got neither because they argued and tried to persuade each other that one was more important.

What do I mean when I say "both"? Well, it is possible to work on two things at once, for example, by reserving the same amount of time at the next meeting. (Or you can form two teams and put each on one task.)

What you need is an action plan on what to tackle first. For now, the task is to prioritize the list and pick three items from your backlog to start on. The process we will use here is a version of a process you did earlier: the selection process.

Step-by-step

The goal is to pick around three items from your backlog. You are not solving them yet. You are just selecting which ones you are spending time and effort on first.

- First, ask everyone if they'd like to include something on the backlog. Maybe there was a new idea or opportunity.
- Now, everyone to (quietly) nominate three items and note them down.
- Everyone shares in a round what items they picked and why. (Nomination round)
- After that first round, ask people if they'd like to change their minds on some of their nominations. (Change round)
- Make a proposal (or ask someone else to make one) of three items to tackle first. Make a good faith effort to represent the energy of the circle.
- Find consent on that proposal. Objections need to point out how the group won't fulfill its aim if the topic is not among

the first three topics addressed. To address objections, you might have to modify, e.g. add a 4th item, or merge items or add a waitlist.

If you have enough time, do a round and see if you can find ways to prepare those agenda items for your third meeting to make sure you can actually make a decision about them. For example, if there are preparatory documents, make sure to share those. Or something needs to be researched (like grants you could apply for), assign it to a person or a group. That way, you're already super prepared next time you meet!

Add new members?

You're almost done! One open question that is still leftover from last time is the question of whether additional people should join your group right now and, if so, who.

To make this decision, first, decide whether you want new people to join at all. The easiest way to find out is to propose:

Proposal:
I propose to select up to ...*x* people to add to the circle.

Follow the typical pattern of presenting the proposal and allowing clarifying questions, quick reactions round, and consent round.

If someone objects – for example, because they worry that the group will be too big or for other reasons – and there is no obvious way to integrate it, let it go and move to the closing.

If everyone consents, you add another quick selection process like in the previous agenda item.

- Ask everyone to decide silently who they will nominate.
- Now ask everyone to share in a round who they picked and why. Since not everyone will know the same people, make sure to give people a chance to ask questions about that person. (Nomination round)
- After that first round, ask people if they'd like to change their minds on some of their nominations. (Change round)
- The facilitator now makes a proposal (or asks someone else to). Whoever picks the proposal makes a good faith effort to represent where the energy is in the circle.
- Find consent. Remind people that if they wanted a person that didn't get proposed this time, it's not a "no forever" but just a "not yet," and that group cohesion and intentional growth are important to start out well.

Note: there are three categories of people who you might want to add:

- People who you know and want in because you think they are a great addition to the group.
- People who you know and you would like to add as the group grows and forms additional sub-groups, for example, because they have expertise in a relevant field.
- People who you don't know yet but who will bring skill sets that you don't have covered in your group.

In this meeting, I would only focus on the first group until you have additional sub-groups or needs.

After the last agenda items, be sure to ask for new ideas for the backlog before you go to the closing round.

Summary table for meeting #2

(See the appendix for a printable version.)

min	Topics	Description
10	Check-in	"How are you?"
5	ADMIN	Attendance, duration, minutes, information, next meeting
5	Consent to agenda	Describe the agenda and ask for consent
30	Topic #1	Selecting roles
10	Topic #2	Infrastructure & communication
15	Topic #3	Gather items for the backlog
15	Topic #4	Prioritize the backlog
5	Topic #5	Add new members? (y/n)
10	Topic #6	(Select new members)
5	Update backlog	Anything you want to flag for later?
10	Check-out	"What was this meeting like?"

Follow-up

- Follow up on all to-dos promised (write them down!)
- Remind the new secretary to send out the minutes
- Remind the new leader and facilitator to plan the next agenda (consulting this booklet!)

6

The third meeting

Meeting overview

By now, you and your group are already very familiar with the format. It will work for all upcoming circle meetings.

Phase	Topic
Opening	Check-in
	ADMIN
Content	Consent to agenda
	Agenda items
	Update backlog
Closing	Check-out

The agenda items for the teal row are:

- Integrate new members (if applicable)
- Form sub-circles, or roles?
- Operationalize priority item #1
- Operationalize priority item #2
- Operationalize priority item #3
- Review processes so far.

The priority items #1-3 are the items that the circle prioritized in meeting #2. (If you selected four priority items, then you now have, accordingly, more agenda items today.)

For all the standard agenda items in grey (check-in, ADMIN, Consent to the agenda, update backlog, and check-out), please refer to the last chapter. Everything is the same, today and forever! (Until you decide to change it..., but how about you stick with it and enjoy the good process forever?)

Integrate new members

If you invited new members to this meeting, do a round where the current members give the new members a short version of who they are. Ideally, you've taken notes the last time, and the new member can read up on the details.

Now let the new member introduce themselves. Take notes. If you want to plan well into the future, make a section in the agenda notes under the backlog and copy the information from the first meeting when people introduced themselves and their previous experiences. Now add to that list the new members' information. Tada! A simple member directory will make onboarding easier until we need something more sophisticated. To comply with privacy laws, find a place where you can store the information.

When the new member has spoken, and you have extra time, make sure people can ask the new person questions; then do a reaction round where everyone can say something to the new person. (Mostly, that's words of welcome.)

Ask for consent to welcoming that person into the circle. By consenting, the incoming member consents to their own membership the circle's aim and the chosen process.

If there are no objections, welcome aboard!

Form sub-circles or roles?

As your circle is launching, this booklet can predict less and less what your group's needs might be. This agenda item gives you

a chance to be intentional on whether you would like to expand your group into subgroups or not. Even if you decide to stay as one group, for now, hear me out because you might need it for the future.

Sub-circles

The idea of circles is to have a perfect fit between people who care about a domain and the circle. If you have noticed that different people have energy in different domains, it might be a good idea to form sub-groups. We don't want that, in a group of eight, three people love to talk about something that doesn't interest the other five. In that case, everyone is much better off if those three people form a sub-group on their sub-topic. Said in another way, we want to create circles where most of the agenda items are relevant for *all* people in the circle. But how do you do that well?

Remember your group's aim? As you grow, that overall aim will turn into the organization's aim. Sub-circles will take on sub-sets of that aim as their sub-circle aim.

The same is true for the domain. If you form a sub-circle, then it is an **empowered** sub-circle. The members of the *sub-circle* then hold the **authority and responsibility** for that sub-domain and *not* your original, general circle anymore. Therefore, clarify what the sub-circle is in charge of (= domain) that *you don't* do anymore.

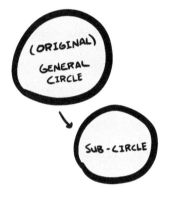

Circle domain:
~~fundraising and~~ funding awards for young transgender and gender-nonconforming artists

Sub-circle domain:
fundraising

In this example, suppose you are a group that has as its aim *fundraising and funding awards for young transgender and gender-nonconforming artists in Western Massachusetts*. In that case, you might want to form a sub-circle that takes care of fundraising, while picking award winners might still remain in the founding circle.

Now that we know that, here's the checklist. To form a successful, semi-autonomous sub-circle, you pass on:

- that part of the aim
- that part of the domain
- plan for membership
- select a leader to link

The full formation of the sub-circle might have to wait. The selections and launching of those sub-circles can happen in subsequent meetings – more on forming subcircles in Chapter 7 on page 79. But in this meeting, you start the conversation.

To do so, ask the group whether they see topics that might be put into a sub-circle. Ideally, you do this in a round or two. After you have heard everyone, you harvest the ideas that emerged. The facilitator might make a proposal (or asks someone to make a proposal), for example, "I propose that we form a sub-circle on the topic XY." You can then put that circle in place right away by defining aim, domain, leader, and a plan on how to populate the circle, or you put "forming XY circle" onto your backlog and continue at a future meeting.

How does one populate a new circle with new members? You can use the selection process very similar to what you have already done: everyone nominates two or three people for the circle; you do a change round and then have a proposal and find consent.

You might choose sub-circle members from among your circle members, or you might add 'new' people from outside the young organization. (My favorite option is to pick 2-3 members for the new circle to form it and then ask the sub-circle to add people of their own choosing. That way, we give them a solid start but also a lot of choice. That sub-circle can add people outside the circle in the same way again as described on page 64.)

In sociocracy, we use linking to get a good flow of information between the circles. The leader of the (sub-)circle serves as 'top-down' link for the new sub-circle.

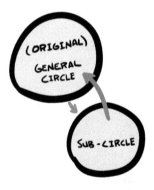

Top-down link to form the circle (leader)

Bottom-up link to securely link the circle (delegate)

Once the new sub-circle circle is up and running, they will confirm that leader by consent (or propose someone else). They will also select a different person as a delegate who will be/stay a member of the original circle. With two people being part of both circles, the two circles are now securely attached and information can flow.

You have created an organism that can now grow limbs – like a cell that is forming new cells!

Roles

What do you do if there is only one person who is interested in working on a topic? In that case, you don't form a whole circle, but you form an operational role. One individual can fill several roles, and they can fill them for a while until someone else fills that role – just like a hat that one person wears for a certain time frame.

In this meeting, identify potential roles and either put them on the backlog or make sure someone writes role descriptions to approve at a future meeting. You will then either propose someone directly (if there's really only one realistic candidate), or you fill your newly defined role for a certain time frame using the selection process.

Complete as much as possible during your meeting. Then add any open steps to your backlog to continue in a future meeting.

The work of identifying topics, interests, and energy, people, and gaps will remain the ongoing work of every circle for as long as the organization exists.

You have now created an organism that can add internal structure – maybe like a cell with organelles. You add as much internal differentiation as you choose to and find useful.

FORMING A SUB-CIRCLE

FORMING ROLES

Operationalize priority item #1

Now how do you turn topics into outcomes?

In general, work is done outside of meetings. Meetings help us create *just enough* clarity and structure so that the work can happen with ease and alignment. In my experience, it's specificity that unleashes energy to act. Creating structure and clarity can mean defining *how* we do things (workflow or policy agreements) or who does them (roles).

Maybe a proposal "falls" out of the brainstorming session. In that case, simply phrase the idea as a proposal and go through the consent process (present the proposal/clarifying questions, quick reaction round, consent).

While forward motion is great, sometimes, it might be that you just bounce ideas in reaction rounds and don't get there within one meeting. Sometimes topics need to marinate a little. That's ok. Just bring them back in the future.

Yet, if you're ready to act but you don't quite have enough specificity and clarity to move forward, below is a robust process that you can use to generate a specific proposal.

Needs statement (optional)

What is the issue you are trying to solve? If the problem you are trying to solve is crystal clear to everyone, do the short version.

Short version: Simply describe the need in a short statement and ask if people are on the same page in describing the need. A *needs statement* might sound like this: "We need to secure funding to support transgender and gender-nonconforming artists in the region."

Longer version: If you would like to explore more, you can follow the process below. You can do each in rounds, with one or two rounds per step.

- Identify what information there is to know about the problem. Share whatever context should be known to everyone.
- What are needs at play here? Who is affected?

- Summarize. The facilitator describes (or asks someone to) the need in one or more sentences and checks whether everyone agrees with that *needs statement*.

(More details can be found in the manual *Many Voices One Song*, section 3.3.2: The three phases of policy process.)

Co-creating a proposal

To generate a proposal, answer these questions, starting with the column on the left, then the middle, and then ask one person to synthesize their ideas from column two into a proposal.

Dimensions	Proposal ideas	Synthesize
What areas do we need to consider? (nouns/questions)	On those areas, what are specific ideas? (*I think we should* statements)	Formulate one proposal from the ideas gathered
• ...	• ...	• ...
• ...	• ...	• ...
• ...	• ...	• ...

See what this could look like for the fundraising question.

Dimensions	Proposal ideas	Synthesize
• fundraising?	For 3 months, pursue grants and fundraising, then evaluate.	• ...
• timeline		
• big/small donors		
• hire someone?	Not hire for now	
• grant writing?	Make a list of potential organizational donors	
• sponsors?		
• other events?	Participate in giving day	

In this case, the proposal ideas in the second column can be put together into a proposal. It will look like magic how quickly you got there! For example, the proposal here could sound like this:

"We will engage in three volunteer-based fundraising activities: (a) make a list of potential organizational donors and reach out, (b) participate in Giving Day event, and (c) pursue other grants. Term: 3 months."

This proposal will then be approved or amended using the consent process in the whole circle.

If the proposal ideas don't converge and align as neatly (or, if some ideas are even contradicting each other), appoint a person or a small team to synthesize the ideas into a proposal, which, again, will be approved or amended in the whole circle.

Just like in the previous agenda item, there is no expectation of completing today. Maybe you make the lists in the first column (dimensions) for each of your three priority agenda items. Maybe you complete one and start the others. It's your choice – together. For time and topic management, the facilitator can make a proposal, for example: "I propose we work on this topic for another 10 minutes and then we start the process for the other two items. Is there anyone who can't work with that?" That way, you can get several things underway at the same time.

Operationalize priority item #2 and #3

In the previous agenda items, you have experienced the process that will now apply to all new items – and carry on forever. You will surface new issues, understand them, explore what needs to be done, come up with a proposal, make decisions, and carry them out. Simply continue for as long as the organization exists.

If you breeze through everything, you might have proposal ideas on all three priority items right away. Consent and start experimenting!

Review the process so far

To adjust to an ever-changing context, any group needs to be resilient. A key feature of resilient groups is to evaluate what they are doing and adapt if needed. To get into that habit, let's do a quick evaluation of processes so far.

Do one round where people can reflect on how the group has been doing, for example, on the following topics:

- Meeting format and facilitation, incl. time management
- Sense of connection
- Pace and progress
- (any other topic)

If issues surface that should be addressed, either address them right away or put them on your backlog. For example, if someone hasn't received emails because their address was inaccurate, fix that immediately. If someone is expressing discomfort with something more general – like gender dynamics in the group – put it on the backlog and make time for it at a future meeting.

Thank everyone for their input, and go to the next item. Do not get dragged into a lengthy discussion here. As a circle, we operate best when we do not always go for instant gratification. The urgent (or urgent-feeling) should not trump the important, and you have consented to an agenda that now requires your attention.

If someone drops a bombshell in the evaluation and the meeting cannot continue, renegotiate the agenda and find consent again.

Warning: you have to make sure there is a balance between building structure (e.g., behavior code or how we divide up the money if we ever make any) and operations. Don't jump into doing when key agreements need to be made first. But also don't get lost in the process when you could also launch pilot projects. The backlog is a great tool to say yes to topics without commitment to address them right away.

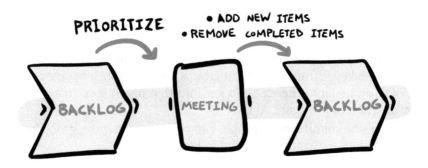

Update the backlog

Now that you've worked on your first backlog items, make sure to update what your backlog says. For example, the question of "how might we secure funding" now gets updated into "make a decision on the funding proposal" if that's what you worked on.

Add all additional ideas and issues, as well as review dates onto the backlog for the future.

Now you simply do this forever! The backlog will be the thread connecting your individual meetings to make sure you are accountable to your own decisions and keep the group focused and coherent.

Check-out

As usual, end the meeting with a check-out. I am sure you are exhausted. That was (again!) a lot of ground covered today!

Make it a habit to become more and more specific and honest in your meeting evaluations. If you don't name them, sub-optimal habits or processes will persist. Name them early, name them gracefully, and put them on the backlog for future problem-solving.

Summary table for meeting #3

(See the appendix for a printable version.)

min	Topics	Description
10	Check-in	"How are you?"
3	ADMIN	Attendance, duration, minutes, information, next meeting
2	Consent to agenda	Describe the agenda and ask for consent
5	Topic #1	Integrate new members
15	Topic #2	Sub-circles, or roles?
20	Topic #3	Operationalize priority item #1
20	Topic #4	Operationalize priority item #2
20	Topic #5	Operationalize priority item #3
10	Topic #6	Review process so far
5	Update backlog	Update the backlog
10	Check-out	"What was this meeting like?"

Follow-up

- Follow up on all to-dos promised (write them down!)
- Remind the new secretary to send out the minutes
- Remind the new leader and facilitator to plan the next agenda (consulting this booklet!)

7

The building blocks of self-governance

Structure, content, review

As a group, you now have all the pieces you need:

- Your backlog holds all open topics.
- Address topics by co-creating and consenting proposals.
- Differentiate and decentralize with roles and sub-circles with aims and domains, membership, links, and delegate.
- With the selection process, select people into roles/circles and pick topics to prioritize.
- As needed, review your processes and surface new topics to improve them over time.

All the rest is just refinement and replication. The building blocks stay the same. Now you can do anything you can imagine!

Ideally, the facilitator and leader prepare the agenda proposal ahead of time. But even if there's no agenda prepared, with these building blocks in place, you can make an *instant agenda* fast:

- Do a round where people say they need to talk about (and whether their proposed item is a report, exploration, or a decision).
- The facilitator turns the suggestions into a proposal and works towards consent.
- Make sure to add all extra topics onto the backlog for future meetings.

How to start a sub-circle

Growth in a decentralized, self-governed organization doesn't happen by growing bigger groups. It happens by growing more circles, just like an organism doesn't grow by having one big cell but by having *many* cells. Similarly, as cells in an organism are formed by another cell for a certain purpose and location, sub-circles are formed by circles for a certain purpose: the aim. As stated above, sub-circles receive the aim as well as their domain from their sub-circle. The parent circle also puts a plan in place on how to populate the new sub-circle intentionally and makes sure there's clarity on how the new sub-circle and the forming circle are linked.

A proposal to form a sub-circle

Let's look at what a proposal to form a sub-circle could look like to give you a good start. For our scenario, let's imagine this is a group of 6 that is meeting for the 5th time following this process. They know their aim, and they have all the roles clear, consent as decision-making, rounds for talking, they defined their circle membership by consent, and they know each other. As an example, let's say this group has as its aim to run an organic and fair-trade tea store in Cambridge. While the original circle is talking about all aspects of this new enterprise (defining their audience, choice, and testing of products, researching suppliers, etc.), they also want to start looking for a physical location of their store. Early on, they had identified *physical location?* as an open topic and put it on their backlog. In the prioritization, this topic ended up pretty high, so now it's on the agenda.

In talking about the topic, they notice that only some of the 6 have strong opinions and interests in this topic while others have more energy around other topics. The opinion forms that this topic best be held by a sub-set of the group because discussing it could easily take up all the available time, and they want the process to start in parallel to planning all the other aspects of the store. So they decide to form a sub-circle.

Here's the checklist for forming a sub-circle from earlier.

- Define the aim of the sub-circle
- Define the domain of the domain
- Define a plan for membership
- Select a leader for linking (and set the expectation that a delegate be selected by the new circle as a backlink)

The group might do rounds in trying to answer these questions until they've pieced together a proposal:

Proposal to form a Location Search Circle.

- Aim: identifying a suitable location for the store.
- Domain: store location
- Membership: Jane and Tahiana as members for now, encouraging them to find more people as needed.

They consent to this proposal and enter a selection process to select a leader for this circle. Knowing that both of them are well-suited, they still settle for Tahiana as the leader for this circle because she has some previous experience. Jane mentions a friend of hers that had offered a few ideas on suitable locations for the store, and they make plans to invite that friend as a new circle member.

Later on, this circle might select Jane or the new person as a delegate to join the parent circle. It is not unusual to have founders like Jane – who is already a member of the parent circle for now – in several linking roles of different circles while the group is still small. As the organization and the sub-circles mature, non-founders will be in new positions more and more. If we spread too fast, our organization might become incoherent and disconnected – grow at a pace that feels refreshing but safe.

Notice that in the domain, it says "store location". If this is approved as the domain as is, the sub-circle will be empowered to *choose* the store location. If this is not what the parent circle wants, it would need to be changed accordingly, for example, to "making a recommendation for a store location (to be approved by the parent circle)". Ideally, sub-circles are empowered to make decisions – that's what decentralized decision making is all about. It is a very common point of tension and misunderstandings, so be sure to be clear exactly what authority you give the sub-circle!

If you would like to see more details and examples for circle structure and linking, please refer to the sociocracy manual *Many Voices One Song*, Chapter 2: Organizational Structure.

Passing on the DNA

In the example of the tea store, the focus was on the mechanics of proposing and populating a sub-circle. In addition to the pure mechanics, we need to talk about culture. You want your organism to grow without turning into a hierarchical, centralized system. To achieve that, each of the parts needs to carry the same DNA as the original circle. By that, I mean: commitment to hearing all voices in consent and in rounds, decentralized authority based on good and transparent information flow through linking and trust.

Given that we are operating in a culture where these values and principles are not the default in organizations, the risk is that we revert to the mainstream culture over time. In my experience, sub-circles often water down the standards until the system becomes unworkable. The only ways to prevent that are to

- set expectations insist that they are kept
- give support in meeting those expectations

If you care about the tools and values in your original circle, make sure they are passed on to all sub-circles.

Let's play with another example for illustration. Let us imagine a group that has formed to achieve the aim of publishing a magazine for care-takers of children with learning challenges. Let's imagine this organization is already somewhat formed (they have several functional circles for different aspects of their project), but now they want to form local chapters in different counties to report on local resources for their audience. They decide to form circles in 3 different counties. How can they make sure those county circles are aligned in their culture and values?

In my experience, the best way to pass on tools and the inclusive culture by committing to practices and living them. In every sub-circle, you need to have at least *one* person who can model by example and support the oncoming members in acquiring the skills and processes.

When forming a sub-circle, you will have at least one person (the selected leader) that has been through several meetings based on self-organization with tools from sociocracy. If this person is willing and able, they can be the *sociocracy guide*, or *self-organization guide* for the sub-circle. (If the leader is not willing and able, make an alternative plan. For example, you could have a second person in the sub-circle hold that role, at least temporarily, or make an effort to train one of the sub-circle members to be that person.)

The next section spells out the first meeting(s) of the sub-circle.

The first sub-circle meeting

The first meeting of a sub-circle is very similar to the founding meeting. It's just a little bit easier because a few parameters are set. Excitingly, the templates you used to form the original circle can also be used for each sub-circle. By default, the leader will facilitate until roles are set or appoint a facilitator following this process.

Looking back at the template for meeting #1, here's how each agenda item translates.

- **Commitment to rounds/consent.** Each circle needs to commit to the DNA of the organization, so it makes sense to commit to rounds and consent as a way to hear everyone in each circle.

- **Decision about the aim/domain.** There is an aim put in place by the parent circle which is very similar to the proposed aim that the convener put in place as the original invitation. The people who are meeting as a sub-circle for the first time need to **accept and affirm that aim and domain as theirs**. This step will ensure that the sub-circle members understand how they fit into the overall organization and what their authorities and responsibilities are.

  Note: the domain of the original circle was "everything". Now with at least two circles in the mix, being clear about each other's domains becomes more important. Be sure to have clarity on what the parent circle will not be in charge of anymore. Having that clarity will help the sub-circle become empowered, responsible and motivated!

- **Experience with regard to the aim.** You might know each other already, but do you know about each other's experience on this sub-aim? This might be easy and brief, but it might make sense to do. For example, you might know each other from an activist context, but if you are forming a Website Circle–do you know each other's website expertise and experience?

- **Getting to know each other.** If you have new members, definitely spend some time getting to know each other. If you already know each other, skip this step.

- **Defining the founding members.** Consent to yourselves and each other's sub-circle membership to formally form the circle. This is a matter of one minute if everything is clear. If it's not clear – for example, because one person isn't sure whether they have time to contribute in the sub-circle – talk about it now!

- **Next meeting.** When are you meeting next? How often do you think your sub-circle should meet?

Depending on how simple the situation is, the template for meeting #1 might be only the first few minutes of the first meeting, and you will move on to the next topics from template #2. Yet, especially if there are a lot of new people, do not rush the beginning. Lack of clarity on the overall aim will catch up with you later. Lack of clarity around process or domains will likely bite you as well!

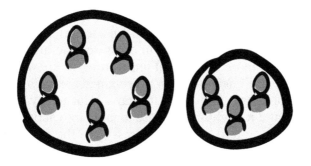

Subsequent sub-circle meetings

How do the agenda items from meeting template #2 and #3 apply to a sub-circle instead of a founding circle?

- **Selecting roles.** This agenda item applies in the same way as in a founding circle. You have a leader (selected by the parent circle), but you need to confirm that leader by consent. Sometimes the person convening the sub-circle doesn't want to be leader beyond forming the circle. In that case, you simply add the leader role to the roles you need to select in a selection process.

  What's different this time is that you also need to select a delegate. (Unlike the founding circle, you have a parent circle to link to!) That means you are selecting a facilitator, secretary, delegate, and maybe a (new) leader.

  Since I am chronically concerned about watered-down commitments around governance, *I'd* make sure that the person who is selected facilitator either is the most sociocratically-experienced person in the room or ask them to follow the processes laid out here. I can only offer this template – but I also know it only becomes lived experience if you choose to *use* it.

  Here's another comment from having seen many of these processes. To become operational as fast as possible, it might seem to take a long time to select roles for the sub-circle. If you are itching to get going, just have the leader make a proposal who could fill which role, put a short term on it (!), and then approve by consent. In doing so, you are missing out on being more intentional and getting to know each other better, and I *definitely don't* recommend skipping full selection processes forever. But there's a lot to say for starting lean, and it might make sense to jump into action fast while committing to do the full process once the first term is up. Setting terms on quick-and-dirty decisions is a great strategy of being fast but intentional. We don't need to figure everything out right away before we can even do a first step.

Instead, we experiment and commit to a timeline of when we will add more groundwork and reflection.

- **Infrastructure and communication.** This agenda item from meeting #2 may or may not apply. You might simply decide to use the same communication system that the parent circle is using. Or maybe you want your own. If things are obvious, make a proposal, consent, and move on. If they are not obvious, take some time to talk.
- **Gather items for the backlog.** This is an excellent practice for any new circle. Gathering topics for later discussion or decision will help the circle get to know each other's priorities and understand what the circle's scope (domain) is in each other's perception. Compiling the list of future agenda items, therefore, is a good tool for alignment, hearing everyone, and making sure we can operate soon and with alignment to the whole.
- **Prioritize the backlog.** Applies just like in the original circle.
- **Add new members? Select new members**. Applies just like in the original circle.

And how about the agenda items from meeting #3? Let's keep this short: they all apply. Simply go back to Chapter 6 on page 66.

In my experience, a sub-circle can be kick-started within one meeting if things are easy and people are experienced. Instead of looking at the templates for the meetings one by one, look at the order of topics. They all build on each other. Go through them step by step while holding a good balance of diligence, pace, and pragmatism. Monitoring your own pace is a skill not unique to starting a self-governed organization, but it's a skillset needed in all phases of your evolution as an organization. Here's what I do: I follow common sense and go as fast as I think we *can* go. Then I slow it down just 10%. Why? Because it's easy to be oblivious and miss pieces or concerns if you go too fast. Having to backtrack when we made a mess costs time. Also, I never compromise on consent – it's our safety net to make sure all voices are ultimately heard.

For reference, see the below list of items to form a sub-circle in the most organic order. Topics #1-10 set up the infrastructure of the circle. You can, of course, revisit and improve those points later.

#1	Commitment to rounds/consent
#2	Decision about the aim
#3	Experience with regard to the aim
#4	Getting to know each other
#5	Decision founding membership
#6	Next meeting/meeting frequency
#7	Selecting roles
#8	Infrastructure & communication
#9	Gather items for the backlog & prioritize
#10	Add new members? | select/integrate new members
#11	Address backlog items
#12	Review processes and policies

Then we enter maintenance mode. At the end of each meeting and whenever issues arise, we gather items for the backlog. As part of that, topics #11 and #12 of addressing backlog items (making decisions and implementing them) and evaluating any decisions we have made (including role performance, policy reviews, etc.) become an ongoing practice as needed or at the end of a term. Forming new sub-circles and roles, selecting people into roles or adding new members are now just part of the backlog items that each circle will address with the regular tools.

To plan a sub-circle meeting, simply wrap the meeting structure around as many agenda items as you think you will cover, and you're good to go!

min	Phase	Topics
5	Opening	Check-in
3		ADMIN
2	Content	Consent to agenda
x		Topics
1		Update backlog
4	Closing	Check-out

To improve your practice, we recommend categorizing your agenda items into these categories:

- Reports: one or more people in the circle have the information they want or need to pass on to the other circle members.
- Explorations: one or more people in the circle have input and would like you to gather ideas or feedback from the circle. In that case, make sure the prompt or question is understood well, and then gather the input in rounds. This is also a good format to brainstorm etc.
- Decisions: either generate a proposal or have a proposal ready. Make sure everyone understands the proposal and gets a chance to react. Then you make a decision.

It is incredibly helpful to know which of these desired outcomes is expected in a meeting. It's a helpful practice to add an R (for report), an E for exploration, or a D for decision to the agenda so that everyone is on the same page and knows what to expect.

I adjusted the time intervals to adjust to a small(er), experienced, and focused group. It's the time frames I use for the circle meetings I facilitate. All the "overhead" sums up to about 15 minutes – a reasonable time frame to make sure the circle is well-connected as human beings, organized as a circle, is tracking items reliably, and adapts and learns over time. Well worth it!

Here are two examples of what an agenda could look like:

min	Topics	Desired Outcome
5	Check-in	
3	ADMIN	
2	Consent to agenda	
10	Approve XYZ role description	D
10	Gathering ideas on conference	E
10	Report from sub-circles and roles	R
15	Decision on webinar workflow	D
1	Update backlog	
4	Check-out	

min	Topics	Desired Outcome
5	Check-in	
3	ADMIN	
2	Consent to agenda	
5	Report on website performance	R
10	Feedback for facilitator	E
10	Reactions to Taru's email	E
10	Review password storage policy	D
10	Selection process for secretary	D
1	Update backlog	
4	Check-out	

The inversion point to decentralization

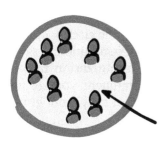

Once you have started several sub-circles, there will be one important movement in your evolution, and we call it the **inversion point**. It's what needs to happen so we can grow as a decentralized organization.

In the beginning, your founding circle is (or was) the *everyone circle*. All original members are automatically part of that *everyone circle*, like a primordial soup of your organization.

As we form linked sub-circles and add new members (the teal dots), we might still have the expectation that the circle in the center is the *everyone circle*. You might even have invited the new members of sub-circles to show up at the *everyone circle* meetings. If you do that or continue to do that, this group will grow and grow in its center, instead of the circles.

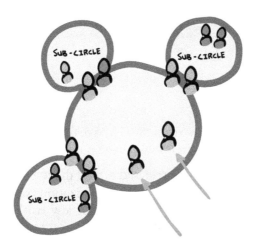

Notice the two members in the middle who are not links from circles, pointed out by the orange arrows.

Now we need an inversion. By a decision in the *everyone circle,* **only leaders and delegates remain in the center circle**, which is now a General Circle to coordinate alignment between the circles to make sure we know and have a way to decide who decides what. Most decisions will now live in the circles, not in the center circle anymore. New members (in teal) will join specific circles and either contribute there or serve as links to the GC in addition to that. **That's when you turn from a centralized organization into a decentralized organization.** If you miss that moment, your group will centralize and form a hierarchy, fade away, or simply not grow.

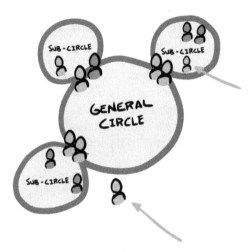

The non-links formerly in the GC have two options if we want to avoid people in work circles who have opinions but don't do work.

(a) They join another circle and attend the meetings there.
(b) They remain members of the organization (stay on the email list, etc.), but they are not part of any work circles. They might attend all-member meetings for input and connection (not for decision-making).

You can select one person in the General Circle (GC) as the leader of the General Circle. This helps create clarity on who is holding attention to the General Circle's well-being. The leader might be one of the leaders and delegates, or an extra person.

Network & community gatherings

After the inversion happens, decision-making is distributed. It no longer resides in the central *everyone circle*, and neither in the General Circle. Instead, each circle takes up their work.

For some initiatives, distributed decision making means that they miss the sense of the whole of being in the *everyone circle*. But this group can still continue! It's just that *decisions* are made in the circles that hold the respective domains. Here are some useful purposes of all-member gatherings.

- During all-member gatherings, circles can ask for feedback and reflections that they then take back into their circle work. Feedback is something very different from making decisions. The feedback becomes input for the circle's decision, allowing the circle to decide based on that input and the circle's own deliberation.

- The people in the all-member gatherings, or the wider network, can also learn together, tell each other their life stories, get sociocracy training, go for hikes together, eat lunch together, talk on forums, show up for Open Space sessions, invite a guest speaker, have cleaning parties, or take anti-racism workshops. These are all activities that can be done well in a large group, inform our work, and enhance our connection with each other. Plan something inviting and establish all-member or network gatherings that fit you. These gatherings can also be useful to recruit new circle members for the operational parts of your work! (For more context, see *Many Voices One Song*, Ch. 2.7.1: Gatherings, interest groups and communities of practice.)

- Connecting with the vision of the organization is an excellent use of time for all-member meetings. Your organization vision and purpose are like a fountain of youth for your operations, for gaining perspective and aligning our thinking. Spend time talking, exploring, reflecting on the vision, and get refreshed and re-connected. If you do not have a declared mission statement yet, it might be a good idea to workshop it now. It will embed the *what* in the *why* of your work and connect you beyond your operations.

Planning long term: the Mission Circle

Over time, you will most likely notice that your organization is great at doing things in many different places, but it lacks vision and long-term planning. That's when you add a Mission Circle.

The Mission Circle consists of some internal members and some external members – those are the people bringing fresh ideas into the organization and serving as a connection to the outside world. You form a Mission Circle in the same way you would form a sub-circle from the General Circle. You decide to form the sub-circle, define what you want it to do, select people from the inside and outside. (We wrote more examples on Mission Circles and who might serve on an MC in *Many Voices One Song*, Chapter 2.5.3.)

In classic sociocratic thinking, the leader of the General Circle is seen as the "top-down" link from the Mission Circle, and the General Circle would add a second, "bottom-up" link from the General Circle to the Mission Circle. No matter how you think about the directions, the leader of the GC and one additional person will make sure the Mission Circle and General Circle are well-connected by having two people who are members of both circles.

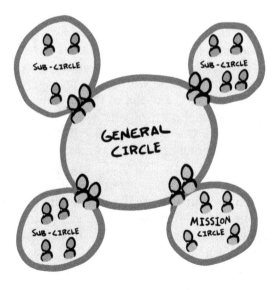

Additional tools: review processes

There are more processes to learn and refine what you do and how you do it. They are listed below. (For all other processes and refinements, please refer to our sociocracy manual, *Many Voices One Song*.)

Policy review

Every policy decision we make need to be reviewed to remain up to date and useful. Typically, we add a review date at the same time we approve the policy, for example after 4 weeks, 6 months or 2 years. To review a simple policy, follow three steps:

Understand
Review the current policy and make sure everyone knows what it says

Explore
Do a reaction round and see what people see that might need improvement.

Decide
Propose an amended policy (with a new term) and seek consent.

Circle review

A circle review is a way to check in on group dynamics and every-one's well-being. Different from a performance review, in the circle review, *everyone* in the group gives feedback to *everyone*. Steps:

1. Focus person #1:

    (a) The first focus person talks about what they did well and what they might want to improve.

    (b) In a round, everyone responds to that focus person and gives feedback on their performance.

    (c) The focus person reflects out loud on the feedback re-ceived.

2. Shift to the next focus person and follow the steps (a) to (c).

3. Repeat until all circle members have had reflection time and have received feedback.

Performance reviews

Performance reviews allow giving detailed feedback to a person in a role. It can be several hours or sessions long, depending on how important it is to the circle. More details are in *Many Voices One Song*, Chapter 4.6 or in our online resources.

- Understand the roles this person is filling
- What has this person done well? (Start and end with the focus person)
- What didn't go so well? (Start and end with the focus person)
- What are the areas of potential improvements, and what are concrete ideas for improvement?
- Write up the concrete ideas into a proposal and seek consent.

Facilitation training

In a review, you might surface that you need more training. I highly recommend getting some facilitators trained and become an even more resourceful, leader-full group. It's hard to overestimate how much good additional training can do. Good meetings smoothen out all the rest, and more training lets everyone participate with ease and shared responsibility.

The biggest points of improvement are integrating objections, and experience on how to not get sidetracked in a meeting. That is outside of the scope of this booklet. We would like to point you to the articles and sample meeting recordings on our facilitation webpage.

As an appetizer, let me highlight here how sociocracy looks at objections.

- The definition of an objection is: something a circle member flags that they believe shows that the proposal isn't safe enough and will harm the circle in achieving its aim. Why would anyone ever object to a proposal? Because they care about the circle and about achieving its aim. Therefore, objections are precious and give you valuable information relevant to your work.

- We make sure to understand the objection. Sometimes we need more information from the person who objected, or ask them to be more specific in explaining their objection.
- As for steps, the facilitator may do a round where people can offer ideas, drawing from those options. Then the facilitation picks what they see as the most promising solution and makes a formal, new proposal. You start again in the consent process and repeat the pattern until there is consent.
- To integrate the objection, there are – at least! – three things you can do. (See list on page 97.)

The right to object needs to be taken seriously because it is essential to the collective steering process. The image I use is one of a boat on a river. The river flows, and we try to stay more or less in the middle of the river, floating along gently. Sometimes we might drift too far to one side, and then we might gently steer back towards the middle. Sometimes, we might not pay attention, or there's a current, then we bump into the banks. It's not a big deal – we simply find our way out again and continue our journey. The gentle steering process is what feedback is. The soft bump into the bank, that's what objections are. We need them to steer.

For example, the right to object to new members is crucial – too many groups have been rendered dysfunctional because of toxic dynamics around individuals. It is also true for consenting to aims or the agenda of a meeting. Consent gives you shared power. You are now 100% responsible and empowered. Use that power!

Modify

Modify the proposal until the proposal is good enough for now.

Shorten term

Shorten the term so you can carry out the proposal and evaluate whether it works. Pick a time frame that seems safe enough.

Measure the concern

Approve the proposal, *and* add tracking concerning the objection. Example: if you are worried about the budget, keep a close eye on how money flows. If you are worried that a policy will confuse customers (therefore harming the aim of delivering service/products to them), find a metric that you could track to make sure you notice immediately if your concerns become true. Move ahead but with your eyes wide open

Your documents

Aims and domains table

As you grow and mature, it will be good to clarify in more detail how you run things. The first important document is the aims and domains table, a written record of who has what authority and responsibility for what in the whole organization. Again, the aim describes what each circle is setting out to do. The domain is a list of "things" each circle has in its domain. As the organization grows and differentiates, aims and domains need to be updated and revised.

Below are aims and domains of a fictional organization with 3 department circles and one sub-circle.

Mission: Sustainable communities and a planet with biodiversity

Org. aim: Fostering permaculture education in ND

Circle	Aim	Domain
General Circle	Ensuring that the department circles operate effectively in alignment with the mission	budget overall
Support Circle	providing, maintaining and improving the infrastructure in XX	membership processes & lists; internal communication
Training Circle	supporting training and consulting delivery on permaculture	all training materials
Outreach Circle	growing the community by increasing awareness of permaculture	website; mailing list
- Social Media	growing the community on social media	social media handles

Governance documents

To protect the governance system that you want to follow for the long run, it makes sense to write it down. Many conflicts in organizations come from a lack of clarity, so create clarity before conflict arises.

There are three different kinds of documents.

- By-laws describe the interface of our organization with the legal sphere.
- Governance agreement: a description of the governance system, for example how policy is made, a description of what consent is, how conflicts are resolved, etc.
- Policies, often collected in a "policy manual" that hold our decisions, e.g. compensation policies, noise policies or whatever is needed to guide the organization's and circles' operations.

You can see see our growing online resources for templates for different sectors, countries, and situations.

8

Now and forever

The main focus of this booklet are the basic patterns of governance and the mechanics of getting a functional, self-governing structure up and running.

In addition, there are other topics you need to pay attention to as you operate, which closely interrelate with governance. The best list of those things to pay attention to that I am aware of are the Core Design Principles phrased by Prosocial, based on the work of Elinor Ostrom.

Prosocial's Core Design Principles.

Wouldn't it be good if someone studied dozens and dozens of co-operatively run organizations all over the world to see what the successful ones do and what the not-so-successful ones lack? Then condense it into a list of criteria and share those? Well, the good news is that it has been done, and done well!

These are the design principles that successful, cooperative organizations are below.

For more information please see www.prosocial.world.

A few comments, also adding a sociocratic perspective are in the below sections.

Core design principles:

1. Strong group identity & understanding of purpose
2. Fair distribution of costs & benefits
3. Inclusive decision making
4. Peer-based monitoring of agreed upon behaviors
5. Graduated responding to behaviors
6. Fair & fast conflict resolution
7. Authority to self-govern (according to CDP1-6)
8. Appropriate relations with other group

CDP 1: Purpose and shared identity

Strong group identity and purpose is what I understand as the mission and aim. As you have seen in this booklet, the aim is the 'initial spark' that makes a group. It's the invitation and the shared, explicitly agreed-upon aim of the group.

Note that any self-managed organization can change and adjust its aim if there is consent.

Yet, it's the purpose that centers all the activity and the choices made. That means that, especially in the long run, every organization needs to make sure that new members are fully aware of the aims of the organization and the circle they are joining. Be sure to add this to your onboarding plan and membership processes.

CDP 2: Fair distribution of costs and benefits

From a sociocratic perspective, these are conversations and decisions that need to be made on a policy level. For example, in a fully formed organization, a membership circle may host the conversation of "what are our expectations of volunteers?" Similarly, in a paid organization, compensation policies have to be worked out with a lot of feedback from all affected people. Be sure to talk about which domains those topics are held in to create clarity and a place where exploration can happen and people can give feedback if they are unhappy with the current status.

If you are forming a volunteer group, creating the domains for financial decisions might be further in the future. If you are starting a business, you need to create that clarity early on.

CDP 3: Inclusive decision making

Using consent and linking, your decision making is probably already above average! The only thing to keep in mind is to make sure information flows well. The circles and consent only affect circle members, but you might have supporting members or simply members of other circles that need to be heard on matters that affect them. The responsibility of every circle includes getting outside feedback.

CDP 4 & 5: Feedback & accountability

Note that I am bundling two different principles here because they go hand in hand quite often. The question here is, how do we share information if something isn't working, and how do we hold people accountable?

Both of these principles are woven into the practice, governance, and culture of our organizations. Sociocratic formats like reviews, selections, and meeting evaluations are wonderful, intentional feedback moments. Yet, it's still people who need to make sure they get scheduled and taken seriously. I always say, meeting evaluations are good moments like sociocracy gives you the stage – but you have to decide to get up there!

In my experience, a commitment to feedback is the hardest principle for people to stick to – they'd rather avoid it. That's why it's good to not only stick to the processes but also, from time to time, renew our commitment to taking in feedback. Feedback is a way to smoothen our collaboration and to re-align ourselves with each other and our new members.

A sociocratic organization needs to be willing to defend its own functioning against inhibiting factors. For example, each circle has to be able to say no to people or even exclude them from a circle. (More about that in the sociocracy manual *Many Voices One Song.*) We need to work into our policies how we hold people accountable if that becomes necessary.

There are small things that make things easier. For example, the backlog is a great way to improve a circle's own accountability, as well as tiny practices like checking who is present and who is filling what role in the ADMIN phase. It's often the small stuff that starts to add up and lets people disengage from the work. Catch it, and improve it.

CDP 6: Fair & fast conflict resolution

Every organization needs its own institutional support of conflict resolution. This is not only practical but also, in my view, a logical consequence of decentralized governance. You have to be able to address conflict in a decentralized way, wherever it might occur. In self-governance, there is no outside source of truth so working things out with each other is key to being and remaining a self-healing organization.

Most sociocratic organizations I know hold the values of restorative justice – connection and support over punishment. Many embrace Nonviolent Communication (NVC). Both tools are based on listening and 100% co-responsibility and shared power. There are great tools out there – use them wisely, use them often! The two aspects here are:

- Personal skills: how well is each individual or group prepared to act when there is conflict?
- Institutional support: What systems does the organization offer overall to support conflict resolution overall?

To start, it's a good idea to define which circle holds the domain of conflict resolution. Then that circle can figure out how to operationalize it for everyone.

In my experience, an organization needs more than one avenue to address this conflict resolution well – but what it might look like highly depends on the context and culture. For example, an organization may make NVC training a requirement before joining or provide ongoing training for members. There might be a role of internal mediators or internal coaching to clarify disagreements before they grow into conflicts. There might be worksheets for internal work, buddy systems, online resources – start with a reasonable and doable solution, implement it, evaluate their effectiveness, and improve from there!

CDP 7: Authority to self-govern

This is an interesting one – and it may not be immediately obvious to you. This core design principle points to the fact that a self-governed organization will struggle if there is too much interference from the outside that the organization itself does not have control over. A good example is legal incorporation and models of ownership. You might never need this with your project, but sometimes it is hard for fully formed organizations to incorporate in a sociocratic way that matches their values. So in a way, it is the legal system that negatively impacts the freedom of a self-governing organization to determine how they want to do things.

For example, what if the law says there has to be a board, and they have to make decisions by majority vote – but the organization wants to make decisions by consent and hold the power in the General Circle and its sub-circles? There are no dealbreakers here, but sometimes a little bit of a workaround is necessary. The same can be said for grant-givers or donors that want to determine how you run things – always make sure to create a context for your organization that gives you as much freedom and flexibility as possible and only adds limitations that you can integrate.

CDP 8: Appropriate relations to other groups

This is more fun! As an organization, not only keep your context-free from negative interferences but also enhance your system with positive influence. For example, form partnerships, coalitions and invite others to be members of your Mission Circle. Meet other groups and keep things open and inviting.

For more information and more ideas on how to keep a tap on these key design principles, see Prosocial's work!

Additional tools

Sociocracy is a governance system, not a magic fix for everyone and everything. There are tons of processes out there that can enhance your practice and complement your governance processes.

There are many good social technologies like Art of Hosting (incl. Open Space), Agile, Lean, Theory U, Permaculture, design thinking, Dragon Dreaming, Acceptance and Commitment Therapy (ACT), The Work, The Work That Reconnects, and the psychological flexibility it brings... the list is long and full of wonderful, holistic practices.

Most of them work best in the realm of surfacing deeper information and more ideas. They can best be used in explorations, for example, to surface possible project ideas or to analyze issues more deeply. In a way, your circle might make a wonderful "excursion" to take a deep dive into a topic using some social technology, and then you turn your output into backlog items (for new ideas to tackle) or proposals (for potential solutions). That's when sociocracy kicks in again to bring the decision over the finish line!

Let the circle be unbroken

I want to share one thought for you as an *oh!*-moment that I owe to my colleague John Buck. Imagine a single circle – like your group of founders.

That circle is like a group of people holding hands – an unbroken circle of people who are working together as equals.

Now, if you add another circle and you have two people (leader and delegate) between this double-linked circle, then the circle of people "holding hands" is still unbroken.

The same is still true even if you add dozens or hundreds of circles. In the image on the right, imagine the dark line was a group of people holding hands. They could all step back more and more until they are forming a big circle – a circle of peers, connected.

We are always one.

Appendix

References

- Atkins, Paul W. B., David Sloan Wilson, and Steven C. Hayes (2019). Prosocial: Using Evolutionary Science to Build Productive, Equitable, and Collaborative Groups. Context Press.
- Buck, John and Sharon Villines (2017). We the People: Consenting to a Deeper Democracy. Second edition. Sociocracy.info.
- Endenburg, Gerard (1998). Sociocracy as Social Design: Its Characteristics and Course of Development, as Theoretical Design and Practical Project. Eburon, Rotterdam.
- Endenburg, Gerard (1998). Sociocracy: The Organization of Decision Making. "No objection" as the Principle of Sociocracy. Eburon, Rotterdam.
- Rau, Ted J. and Jerry Koch-Gonzalez (2018). Many Voices One Song. Shared power with sociocracy. Sociocracy For All.
- Rosenberg, Marshall (2003). Nonviolent Communication: A Language of Life. 2nd edition. PuddleDancer Press.

Resources

Next following pages contain facilitation notes alongside with meeting agendas. Please see the website

www.sociocracyforall.org/whodecides

to find digital, updated versions of these printables plus more shareable resources in support of this book.

#1 Meeting agenda

 Sociocracy Fo

time	min	topic	
0:00	15	Check in	
0:15	5	Attendance Duration Information	
0:20	5	Consent to agenda	
0:25	10	Commitment to consent	D
0:35	10	Commitment to rounds	D
0:45	20	Decision about the aim	D
1:05	10	Experience with regard to the aim	E
1:15	15	Getting to know each other	R
1:30	10	Defining founding members	D
1:40	5	Next meeting	D
1:45	5	Update the backlog	
1:50	10	Check out	

www.sociocracyforall.org/whodecides

Notes for facilitators

In a round, everyone shares who and how they are. *"How are you doing entering the meeting?"*

- Notice who is present/missing/late.
- Make sure someone is taking notes.
- Ask for permission to facilitate (or ask someone else to facilitate and get the group's permission)

Mention the duration of this meeting. Is everyone able to stay until the end of the meeting?

Ask if anyone has any information to share, like an announcement, an invite, or a celebration.

(1) Describe the agenda and make sure people can ask questions for understanding.
(2) Ask whether something needs to be changed or if the agenda is good enough to get started.

Use the consent process ↓ for this proposal. *"We commit to consent as a decision-making method"*

Use the consent process ↓ for this proposal: *"We commit to rounds as a default way of talking, in particular for check-ins and check-outs, most explorations, and for consent rounds."*

Use the consent process ↓ for the proposed aim.

Ask, "when you think about this project with the aim (...), what do you bring as a resource, like previous experiences, connections, contacts, and resources?"

Do a round of sharing. "What are you passionate about?" or: "What was your path to get here?"

(1) Explain that all members of the group need to consent to be "in" on the aim and with each other.
(2) Ask everyone to indicate whether they want to be part of the group.
(3) Ask for consent from everyone "in" to everyone also indicating they wanted to be members.
(4) If there are no objections, you are now a circle with members!

Make a date, or assign the task of scheduling to someone.

If you have come across open questions or topics that need more exploration, write them on the backlog - your list of open topics for future meetings.

Ask "What did you enjoy in this meeting that we should do again? And what would improve your experience?" Take notes - if there are specific ideas or issues, add them to the backlog.

Consent process

(1) **Clarifying questions:** Read the proposal and make sure people can ask questions for understanding.
(2) **Quick reactions:** One round for people to share thoughts and opinions.
(3) **Consent:** Ask whether there are objections to the proposal.

No objections: the proposal is approved! If there are objections, integrate the wisdom they bring by doing rounds of exploration. You might modify, add/change its term, track the impact, etc.

#2 Meeting agenda

 Sociocracy Fc

time	min	topic	
0:00	10	Check in	
0:10	5	Attendance Duration Minutes Information Next meeting	
0:15	5	Consent to agenda	
0:20	30	Selecting roles	D
0:50	10	Infrastructure & communication	D
1:00	15	Gather items for the backlog	E
1:15	15	Prioritize the backlog	D
1:30	5	Add new members (y/n)	D
1:35	10	(Select new members)	D
1:45	5	Update the backlog	
1:50	10	Check out	

Roles

Leader:
Making sure the circle runs and is operating.
- Checking in with people and tasks
- Notice items that are falling through the cracks and either deal with them or bring them to the circle.

Facilitator:
Making sure the circle meetings run.
- Planning the agenda (with input from the leader) and inviting members.
- Holding circle meetings.

Secretary:
Making sure the circle's documents are in order.
- Taking notes during circ meetings.
- Making sure minutes ar other related documen are accurate and up to

(You might later add a dele

Notes for facilitators

 Sociocracy For All

In a round, everyone shares how they are. *"How are you doing entering the meeting?"*

- Notice who is present/missing/late.
- Make sure someone is taking notes.
- Ask for permission to facilitate (or ask someone else to facilitate and get the group's permission)

Mention the duration of this meeting. Is everyone able to stay until the end of the meeting?

Are the meeting minutes accurate? Were they distributed? Do all members have access?

Does anyone have any information to share, like an announcement, an invite, or a celebration?

Confirm your next meeting date/time or make a plan.

(1) Describe the agenda and make sure people can ask questions for understanding.
(2) Ask whether something needs to be changed or if the agenda is good enough to get started.

Use the **selection process** ↓ to select a leader, facilitator and secretary

Use the consent process for an infrastructure proposal (see book)

What are topics you will have to talk about, issues you might have to solve? In rounds, let people collect future agenda items. You can prompt them by asking "How might we...?"

(1) Add items to the backlog. (2) Let everyone identify 3 items they find important (3) Everyone shares in a round which items they find most important. (4) Do a second round where people can respond or change their priorities. (5) Make a proposal and find consent.

Do you want to add members? To test, propose to add additional members. If someone objects and there is no obvious way to integrate it, move on. If everyone consents, go to the next item.

Use the **selection process** ↓ to select a new circle members. One modification: this time, your nominations are people from outside of your circle.

Make sure all additional future topics are written onto the backlog.

Ask "What did you enjoy in this meeting that we should do again? And what would improve your experience?" Take notes - if there are specific ideas or issues, add them to the backlog.

Selection process

1) **Review the roles**
2) **Gather qualifications for each role.**
   In rounds, compile a list of qualifications and qualities for each of the roles that a person filling that role should have.
3) **Consent to the list of qualifications.**
4) **Let everyone nominate (silently).**
   Remind everyone that they can nominate themselves!

(5) **Share nominations & reasons (round)**
(6) **Change round**
   Give everyone a chance to change their nomination. It is not necessary that everyone nominates the same people by the end!
(7) **Make a proposal and go to consent.**
   You can either make a proposal yourself or ask someone else to make one.

If there are objections, use the strategies of integrating objections from the consent process.

#3 Meeting agenda

 Sociocracy F

time	min	topic	
0:00	10	Check in	
0:10	3	Attendance Duration Minutes Information Next meeting	
0:13	2	Consent to agenda	
0:15	5	Integrate new members	D
0:20	15	Sub-circles, or roles?	D
0:35	20	Operationalize priority item #1	D
0:55	20	Operationalize priority item #2	D
1:15	20	Operationalize priority item #3	D
1:35	10	Review process so far	E
1:45	5	Update the backlog	
1:50	10	Check out	

Notes for facilitators

 Sociocracy For All

In a round, everyone shares how they are. *"How are you doing entering the meeting?"*

- Notice who is present/missing/late.
- Make sure someone is taking notes.
- Ask for permission to facilitate (or ask someone else to facilitate and get the group's permission).

Mention the duration of this meeting. Is everyone able to stay until the end of the meeting?

Are the meeting minutes accurate? Were they distributed? Do all members have access?

Does anyone have any information to share, like an announcement, an invite, or a celebration?

Confirm your next meeting date/time or make a plan.

(1) Describe the agenda and make sure people can ask questions for understanding.
(2) Ask whether something needs to be changed or if the agenda is good enough to get started.

If you invited new members, let them introduce themselves. Decide by consent to accept them.

In rounds, see whether there are sub-circles or roles you could establish in the near future.

Use the policy process ↓ to address your priority item.

Use the policy process ↓ to address your priority item.

Use the policy process ↓ to address your priority item.

Do one round where everyone can take the big-picture view. How has this process worked for us? What would we like to do differently, for example on meeting format, facilitation, time management, our sense of connection with each other, and any other relevant topic.

Make sure all additional future topics are written onto the backlog.

Ask "What did you enjoy in this meeting that we should do again? And what would improve your experience?" Take notes - if there are specific ideas or issues, add them to the backlog.

Policy process

(1) **Understand the issue**
- What is there to know about the issue?
- What are needs at play here? Who is affected?
- Synthesize into a needs statement and see if everyone consents to it.

(2) **Create a proposal by...**
- **identifying the dimensions**
("In order to make a good agreement, we will have to say something about ___")
- **gathering proposal ideas**
("I think we should ___")
- **synthesizing the proposal ideas into a proposal**

Once there is a proposal, seek consent in the consent process.

#n Meeting agenda

time	min	topic	
0:00	5	Check in	
0:05	3	Attendance Duration Minutes Information Next meeting	
0:08	2	Consent to agenda	
0:10	x	Topic #1	RED
0:xx	x	Topic #2	RED
0:xx	x	Topic #3	RED
0:xx	x	Topic #4	RED
1:xx	x	Topic #5	RED
1:xx	x	Topic #6	RED
1:xx	3	Update the backlog	
1:xx	5	Check out	

Fill in topics from the backlog.

Is the topic a Report, Exploration, or Decision?

www.sociocracyforall.org/whodecides

Notes for facilitators

In a round, everyone shares how they are. *"How are you doing entering the meeting?"*

- Notice who is present/missing/late.
- Make sure someone is taking notes.
- Ask for permission to facilitate (or ask someone else to facilitate and get the group's permission).

Mention the duration of this meeting. Is everyone able to stay until the end of the meeting?

Are the meeting minutes accurate? Were they distributed? Do all members have access?

Does anyone have any information to share, like an announcement, an invite, or a celebration?

Confirm your next meeting date/time or make a plan.

(1) Describe the agenda and make sure people can ask questions for understanding.
(2) Ask whether something needs to be changed or if the agenda is good enough to get started.

Reports: (1) Present and let people ask clarifying questions

Exploration: (1) Present the issue, let people ask clarifying questions
(2) Let people give their ideas or reactions

Decisions: (1) Present the proposal, let people ask clarifying questions
(2) Let people give their ideas or reactions
(3) Ask for consent/objections

Make sure all additional future topics are written onto the backlog.

Ask "What did you enjoy in this meeting that we should do again? And what would improve your experience?" Take notes - if there are specific ideas or issues, add them to the backlog.

CPSIA information can be obtained
at www.ICGtesting.com
Printed in the USA
JSHW021351051222
34309JS00003B/15